MW00654850

UNBURDENING SOULS

AT THE SPEED OF THOUGHT

Psychology, Christianity,
and the Transforming Power
of EMDR

by

Dr. Andrew J. Dobo

Soul Psych Publishers
Florida

Copyright ©2015 by Dr. Andrew J. Dobo

All rights reserved. No part of this book may be reproduced or transmitted in any form or by any means, electronic or mechanical, including photocopying, recording, or by any information storage and retrieval system, without permission in writing from the writer and publisher.

Published by Soul Psych Publishers, LLC

Learn more about the author and EMDR at AndrewDobo.com

Cover illustration by Nicole Bateman

ISBN: 978-0-9962207-0-5

First edition

For Jo

Table of Contents

Foreword

This book is not a "how to" manual. It does not explain exactly how EMDR, a swift and effective but little-known form of psychotherapy, is done.

It does seem important for the reader to know a little about the process, but this book is about the activation of the soul. EMDR gives access to the person's higher self. It opens a portal to inner wisdom by shutting down the ego and intellect. This is no small thing. Monks meditate in silence for years to get to a place of wisdom that EMDR can get to in moments.

EMDR is always done with an image, a memory of a wounding event, and the negative thought that resonates with that event. EMDR aligns the heart with what the head knows to be true. The intellect cannot cure these wounds, but we can heal them with EMDR.

Psychology rejects religion, for the most part, and religion rejects psychology. In this book I attempt to unite the two.

A final note: All identifying information of these cases has been changed to protect the client's identity. Sometimes the age has been changed, the sex of the client is sometimes changed, where they were from or what they looked like. If I mention children that is usually not accurate. The "who" this has happened to is unimportant; the thing that is important is "what" happened. I again am very grateful to all of my clients who allowed me to share parts of their stories.

I

A Glimpse into the Healing

Georgia was ready, so we began. In less than fifteen seconds, she began to shiver, to shiver as if she had just been dragged out of an icy river in the middle of winter. The temperature in my office was a comfortable seventy-five degrees. Her teeth began to chatter, her cheeks started to turn red, and after a minute or two, her lips turned a little blue.

Nine or ten years ago, this reaction might have caused me some anxiety, but I had become accustomed to these kinds of dramatic displays when I used the eye movement therapy known as EMDR in my therapeutic work. I had had to learn to tolerate the intensity of these moments, but I still lamented that my patients must revisit their horrors yet again, as if living them was not punishment enough.

The first patient who had displayed a dramatic explosion of emotion was Suzanne, some ten years earlier. She had had a horrible childhood. When I first started working with her, she was sixty-two years old. She was attractive, very intelligent and insightful, but still tormented and broken by a mother long since dead.

"Mother," as she called her, never "mom," was evil.

There is really no other way to put it.

Suzanne was successful in her career. When I saw her, she had earned a master's degree and was working as a project manager in an IT firm. Given her history, it was a miracle that she had accomplished so much. When she had been a child, her mother had almost killed her on dozens of occasions.

"Mother's recreation was torturing me," she said. "She hated me, and I knew it in utero. I was a difficult birth, because I remember not wanting to be born to this woman." It did not matter if this was true or not. It was her truth, and I accepted it as the truth. Also, she described experiences she had had when she was in this woman's womb with such clarity that I believed her.

Her father had read the paper during episodes when her mother tortured her, or just watched and did nothing. He intervened only once.

"Mother," he said, "You're going to kill the poor girl." He felt the wrath of mother for months after making that single statement, and so did Suzanne.

Mother had said: "You think I'm going to kill the poor girl? Watch this!"

One of her mother's favorite torments had taken place at dinner. She regularly grabbed the little girl by the back of her neck and shoveled food and milk down her throat. Suzanne would choke, gag, and eventually pass out, after which she would wake up sweaty and alone in her bed with her Mickey Mouse T-shirt and her face covered with milk and remnants of peas, having no recollection of how she got there. These episodes happened dozens of times and went on for years.

Suzanne was the first patient I treated who expressed extremely violent emotional discharges during EMDR sessions. In the early sessions with her, I acted as if I was accustomed to this process, but in reality I was terrified, saying to myself: "Holy shit! What am I supposed to do now?" I had read about these kinds of dramatic events and had been told about them in training, but I had never witnessed any like hers.

Suzanne's outbursts could last an hour or more. She was usually exhausted but relieved after these sessions. She felt an enormous amount of pent-up horror that she had kept locked up for fifty-plus years. Once each EMDR session began, the emotion came spewing out like a dormant volcano finally permitted to erupt, and erupt it did, as quickly and as powerfully as she could endure.

I began to rethink my role when working with heroic people like Suzanne. I witnessed the incredible transformation that happened to her and, later, to many others who came to see me for EMDR.

The difference between using EMDR and ordinary psychotherapy was that with EMDR, there seemed to be a fast and complete transformation of the personality. By fast, I mean months, not years. For example, after a few months, Suzanne was happy. She felt safe for the first time in her life. I could not believe what was happening to her, nor was I sure exactly how or why it was happening. I knew that I had a small role in it, but I was not sure what exactly I was doing and what exactly was happening to cause such incredible transformations.

I recently read Jungian analyst and author Robert Johnson's biography, *Balancing Heaven and Earth.* He says that things go best for him when he reminds himself that "I have no idea what is going on in the person and that I have no special wisdom to impart."[1] Humility is always a better choice than egotism.

There are visionaries in Medjugorje, a small village in Bosnia, who claim to speak to the Blessed Virgin Mary. They often ask for healings for people, and the Virgin Mary says: "I cannot heal; only God can. I need your prayers and sacrifices to help me."[2] Her statement makes Robert Johnson's words even more relevant. I was nothing in this process. Yet the changes were dramatic and stable in the lives of people like Suzanne.

She had an important dream as we began to close our work together. It was important for her in that it reflected the transformation she had undergone, and it was important for me in that this single dream began to change the way I saw my clients.

Suzanne dreamt that she found a beautiful leather-bound blue book with the title written in exquisite gold script. The title of the book was *Sometimes in Death a Friend You'll Find.* All I could say to that was, "Wow!" as I tried to hide the goose bumps that were running up and down my arms from such a profoundly important title.

This dream was one of those that got me to consider the EMDR process as a death and rebirth sequence: a

Jungian view that I had personally experienced, a transformation process that I knew to be true. But no such terminology had ever been used in my graduate training, so I had stifled this kind of thinking, even though it had literally saved my life.

Suzanne's dream encouraged me to think about my work in a mythic rather than scientific sense. I accepted the title of "friend," as the dream had suggested, rather than "doctor," although not in all cases and not all the time. This, and other dreams clients shared with me, brought me to my understanding of the six stages of therapy, as you will see, but hers was the first nudge toward my new, yet old, way of thinking. I was beginning to shake off the shackles of my training and think for myself.

These changes in Suzanne were far more comprehensive and complete than just getting over a trauma. Everything was changing for the better in her life. She was grateful, but I did not feel as if I had much to do with it. I just sat there and watched it happen.

EMDR is very different from most kinds of therapy. During EMDR, there is little talking and no reassuring. Clients must surrender to the process to be healed. If you had lived with evil for years, learned you could trust no one, and a therapist said, "This works, but you have to allow yourself to briefly re-experience these horrors to be healed and free of them," you might understand why they say: "Fuck you, doc! I'm not doing that."

This moment of denial, when they refuse to make the journey, is the first stage of the Christian Passion experience that clients go through in EMDR. They're in my office because a part of them received an invitation. Once the invitation is accepted, there is no turning back. The soul will not be denied its true path of wholeness and healing.

What does denial of the journey have to do with the Christian Passion? It is the beginning of the Passion of Christ — Gethsemane. Christ expressed a similar denial himself. "And going a little farther he fell on his face and prayed, saying, 'My Father if it is possible, let this cup pass from me.' "[3] (Matt: 26:39-40) Christ did, however, surrender to his reality, as we all must.

This is the first stage of the six stages related to the crucifixion of Christ that occurs with EMDR: The client must endure a psychological crucifixion. With EMDR, the patient has a psychological reenactment of Christ's journey. EMDR does not simply treat symptoms, it dismantles the old self that is no longer working, to make way for the new self. Only in death (psychological death) a friend you'll find.

I helped Suzanne to heal and become whole. For example, she began to have enough trust to date men again. She had lived alone and isolated for years, but now she was feeling more confident and relaxed.

I'm not sure who benefited more from our work together, she or I. I've done more than twelve years of daily EMDR work helping trauma victims recover and heal since Suzanne ended treatment. Many tears have been shed in my little second-floor office that overlooks palm trees and the Intracoastal Waterway here in Florida.

꙳

Georgia, still shivering in my office, had been molested by her father most of her life. She had escaped by using drugs and alcohol. Her mother hated this daughter and physically abused her because her husband preferred Georgia to her. To make matters worse for Georgia, her father showered the child with gifts that created envy in her brothers. He took her on vacations to their cabin for "fishing" trips, leaving her brothers at home.

She begged him to take her brothers instead or at least bring them along, but no. As you might expect, her brothers' hatred for her grew. They attacked her physically and emotionally at every chance. To say she was shivering and "left out in the cold" would be an understatement.

Oh, yes, dad was a big man in the church, a respected elder. The whole community loved the guy. Amazingly, she did not blame God but attended her church regularly.

Georgia's story changed me. It was not more horrifying than other stories I had heard over the years, but for some reason, after experiencing her shivering session, after watching her in my office wailing, balled up in a fetal position on the floor in front of me, I was not the same.

After this grueling session, which was one of hundreds, perhaps even thousands, that I had facilitated and witnessed over the years, I went home, made a drink, and wept. This had never happened to me before. I could usually leave my work at the office, but not on this day. I had heard hundreds of these horror stories but never dwelled on them, because I was trained not to. This night, however, a client's pain got the best of me.

It was a night of tears, a night of recall, a night of seeing images of the stories I had heard over the past decade. It was a seemingly endless flood of horrible pictures running through my head at the speed of light, pictures from stories that had been shared in my office these past ten years — one flash after another and another. It was as if I was doing EMDR without doing EMDR, hearing all of these horrors of molestation, physical abuse, and beatings — many stories where the parent brought the child to the verge of death.

After the flood ended, I was exhausted, my face soaked with tears. I asked myself, "Why on earth would God want to have anything to do with humans?" I would have thrown in the towel on humanity long ago. How could these parents hate their children so?

I was naïve. I had no idea how frequently parents tortured their children. I learned quickly. It happens everywhere and all the time. It happens with the wealthy and the poor, the bright and the dumb. It happens. I would often ask myself, "Why was I so lucky in my childhood, blessed with my simple and loving family?"

During this heavy-laden night, for some reason, I remembered a prayer that I learned as a child. One line kept playing over and over in my head, "To thee we send up our sighs, mourning and weeping in this valley of tears." I did not know how much longer I could live in this valley of tears, which felt like an ocean of sadness created by evil and madness. Day in and day out, I heard stories of adults who as children lived in the midst of evil. On this night all I could think was: "The valley of tears. I work in a valley of tears."

This was a different sadness than I had ever felt before. I had lost a father whom I loved, and other family members. I had known grief and sadness, but this was different. I wasn't sure what to make of it. I later met with a colleague and friend, my EMDR therapist. We talked about this sadness for a while, and I did EMDR, which, as always, helped dramatically. She still checks up on me to make sure I'm taking care of myself, which I am.

She said: "You know, Andy, we work with EMDR in a very emotionally charged way. You have to take time off, take care of yourself. There's no chitchat in our work. It is deadly serious business."

A few days after my tearful episode, I ran into one of my graduate school professors, another friend and mentor. He had first taught me how to use EMDR back in the 1990s. I shared my experience of this episode of sadness with him.

He was always one with a story. He had spent most of his career treating Vietnam Veterans with PTSD and doing research with this group. He said, in his soft voice and subtle Southern accent, "Did I ever tell you 'bout the time I was pickin' up leaves out by the pool?" He always told great stories, and I thought I had heard them all more than once, but to my surprise I had not heard this one.

"No," I replied.

"I was sittin' out by the pool with my wife, and I started pickin' up leaves, one at a time. I would get up, pick up a leaf, and bring it to where I was sittin'. Then I'd sit for a few minutes and do it again, and again. I did this about ten times. My wife said to me, 'What the hell are you doing?'

"I didn't really know what I was doing, but I said to her without hesitation, in a voice deep with sadness, 'I'm pickin' up wounded and broken soldiers,' and I wept, too, Andy. I wept, too. You make sure you take care of yourself with this work."

I guess I know why God does not give up on humans. He doesn't give up on us because of people like my dedicated professor, like my colleague and therapist, and because of the wounded, tortured souls who do not give up on themselves.

He doesn't give up on humans because of the victims, who despite their unanswered prayers for salvation still love God. Or perhaps they may hate God, and I think God understands. The distinguished American author and activist Robert Bly explains this struggle when he quotes from ancient wisdom in *A Little Book on the Human Shadow*. He says, "If one loves and worships God he may come to an understanding of Him in twenty or thirty years, but if he hates God he can do the same work in two years."[4]

Not all of the people I have treated love God, as you might imagine, and perhaps rightfully so. Some hate God because they felt so abandoned by Him, and by everyone else for that matter, as they endured a life of torment completely alone and betrayed.

Even after their abuse has long since ended, the torment continues for the victims. Even with the perpetrator long since dead or jailed, the torment continues for the battered. Even with the war long since over, the torment continues for the veterans.

I hate having to ask these people to relive their horror. Believe me, I think they have endured enough. I wish there was another way, but I know of no other. I would never invite them to take this journey if I wasn't sure it would transform them and bring them peace. I know it's the best shot they have.

I'm not sure when my view of my work began to change. It was a slow process. I stopped seeing my patients as clinical entities. St. Gregory stated, "A soul in trouble is near to God."[5] I started to see my clients as souls in trouble, and to sense that they were indeed near to God, even though they often did not feel it. They often seemed to be in a holy battle, a Herculean struggle. I started to see them as heroes who had far more resilience and courage than I could ever imagine.

They were far more than patients with symptoms. In fact, in this book I will never refer to them as patients, nor will I talk about symptoms or treatment. A million books about therapy are out there, and this is not one of them.

I stopped feeling like a psychologist but instead like a guide or companion, and near the end of the process, more like a midwife who would assist the person through his or her darkness into a new life, a midwife of rebirth. Every person would endure this psychological crucifixion. Their old selves would have to die for the new selves to be born. This is a very painful and emotional experience and, for this to happen, I have to earn their trust. They have to have confidence in me. They have to feel safe. Most of them have no idea how to do any of these things. They have never trusted anyone. They don't even know what it feels like to know someone whom they can trust.

At times I felt compelled to pray. Once the need to pray started, the change became more profound for me. I prayed for them while they were in agony. I fasted for them and began to feel a much greater and deeper empathy for them. Once I started to pray, the work became holy for me, not dry or sterile, but sacred, holy, and mystical.

Of course they were unaware of all of this. This is the first time I have ever mentioned my praying to anyone. I never imagined I would pray in my office or fast on bread and water for people in the hopes of easing their very heavy burdens. They don't teach you this in graduate school. There's a lot they don't teach you there.

It just seemed as if there was nothing else for me to do. With EMDR, these heroes go it alone. I set up the process and just watch to make sure they're safe. I say no words of wisdom; I just shut up and allow them to go back into their pain, ironically, to be free of it. I do what I can, which isn't much, and I pray.

I stopped thinking about the person's family of origin as dysfunctional. It was not simply a "dysfunctional family system," but a place where evil resided and set up shop to destroy lives and souls. I would often feel rage well up within me against these perpetrators. Sometimes it was hard to shake this rage. I experienced evil by proxy, and the more I heard, the more I hated.

Somewhere in the transformational work with a number of these people I began to notice a parallel between the transforming power of EMDR and what C.G. Jung, the founder of Jungian psychology, describes as the "individuation process." Jung suggests that individuation is a never-ending movement of the self to change and grow throughout the lifespan. Of course, one can decide to avoid this process altogether and learn nothing new throughout a lifespan. One does not have to look very far to encounter people who seem to have learned nothing about themselves, or about anything else for that matter.

EMDR manifests the Jungian model of the psyche, or, if you will, it activates the soul. It accelerates the individuation process. EMDR is like Jungian depth psychology on steroids. It moves very fast, and changes in a person's life occur quickly.

More importantly, the transformational work with EMDR perfectly mimics the Passion of Christ that Jesus of Nazareth modeled. Jung talks about these stages without mentioning Christ. I am bravely, or perhaps foolishly, going to talk about God throughout this book, identifying the six Christian stages and how they manifest themselves in this work.

My goal here is to help you, the reader, to view psychology as the rich and powerful process that it is. Perhaps you will see it as the sacred work that I am privileged to do. When someone says, "No one knows this, not even my husband," the words that follow this statement are sacred and privileged, usually revealing a rape or molestation that is a secret deeply hidden. This is deadly serious work. I hope that you will see just how brilliant Jesus of Nazareth was, in that his words and his model work and touch us on multiple levels. This book is about the psychological relevance of his life and death.

Georgia began the shivering session just like most EMDR sessions. She sat in the chair in front of the light bar, which is an approximately two-foot-long horizontal bar where a row of blue lights rapidly glides back and forth in a straight line from one end to the other. Georgia had to keep her head still and only move the pupils of her eyes back and forth, tracking the lights as they moved.

She also held the oval tactile stimulators, one in each hand, one gray and the other black, both tethered to the base of the light bar by a wire. These stimulators gently vibrated alternately in her hands, always in unison with her eye movements. When her eyes looked left, the gray stimulator in her left hand vibrated. When her eyes looked right, the black stimulator in her right hand vibrated. The hand devices made it possible for her to close her eyes during EMDR if she felt compelled to do so.

I have seen many strange things happen during EMDR sessions, especially when the body is greatly involved in the process. One of my EMDR trainers shared the story of a forty-five-year-old male client whom he was treating. They targeted an old memory of how the man's father had taken him for a haircut when he was six years old. The client was afraid of the barber and was usually taken for a haircut by his mother, who was much more understanding with her son than the father was.

On this occasion, the boy was crying in the barber's chair. The father decided to shut the boy up by slapping him across the face. The client recalled the incident clearly, and he stated that he could see his father's hand print on his little six-year-old cheek in the mirror as the barber cut his hair.

When this memory was targeted using EMDR, this forty-five-year-old man's cheek began to turn red, with a clear imprint of fingers on it. EMDR seeks and finds the path of the imprinted memory and dismantles it.

Extraordinary sights like this imprint of fingers and other astonishing reactions appear when clients do EMDR. I have had clients say they are speaking to God, and I have watched the chairs clients are sitting on bounce and rock. I have seen other clients like Georgia, whose emotions and memories are so painful that they will wail and end up on the floor in a fetal position. These are common occurrences in EMDR, but Georgia's emotional response was one of the most dramatic scenes I'd ever witnessed.

When Georgia walked into my office, it marked my tenth year of trauma work with EMDR — ten years in a busy practice, hour after hour of hearing horror story after horror story, and witnessing the intense pain of these people.

A friend once said to me, "How can you listen to people whine all day?" I was speechless. One of the reasons I'm writing this book is to dispel the idea that therapy is for weak people. Therapy is for the courageous. Anyone can avoid him or herself, but not many people have the courage to open up their souls to see their deepest, darkest reality. No. They prefer to call my clients "whiners."

John Sanford, a Jungian analyst and Episcopalian minister, says that those who are brave enough to seek out therapy and work through a process of individuation are people invited into the Kingdom of God. He writes: "Precisely those who seem the least fit for the kingdom are those who come to enter into it. Those who are forced by life to concede to themselves that they are psychologically crippled, maimed, or blind can be compelled to enter into the great feast. But those who are convinced that they are self-sufficient do not enter because they remain caught in their own one-sidedness."[6]

I remember the first day Georgia walked in my office. She said: "Five years. I can last five years. If this EMDR doesn't work, I'm going to kill myself in five years. My daughter should be on her own by then."

I refuse to treat clients who threaten me with suicide. Their idea is that if I can't fix them, they're going to kill themselves. They have to find some other fool to accept that Devil's bargain. With Georgia, though, five years was a long time. She also had had EMDR in the past with good results, so I took a chance, and so did she. It worked out.

On that day of breakthroughs, it had been months since that initial meeting. She was in an emotional storm. She began crying and wailing. Heaving, with chattering teeth and shivering body, she sobbed out loud, so loudly that the white noise machine was no match for the discharge of her intense emotional outburst.

Finally, after five or six minutes of my watching her, she seemed to have a reprieve. I asked, "What are you noticing?" This may seem like a lame comment in the midst of high drama, but it's what we are trained to say. We are trained to stay out of the way and trust the process. I did, and I do trust it.

"What are you noticing, Georgia?" I asked again, softly and compassionately.

"I'm in the snow. I'm five years old and my mother threw me out in the snow in my pajamas after beating me. It's freezing. I'm freezing."

I said, "OK, go with that," and she continued. The shivering and sobbing continued for another two or three minutes, and then a brief reprieve came.

Again I asked, "What are you noticing?"

"My dad's in his workshop behind the house. He makes furniture there."

"OK, go with that — the workshop."

She immediately began to shiver and sob again, only this time the sobbing was even more intense, almost unbearable, to the point where she could not sit in the chair any longer. She slid off the chair and was now in a fetal position on the floor, sobbing, wailing, heaving, and shivering. She stayed on the floor for almost twenty more minutes.

In such intensely painful moments, I feel helpless, just sitting there and watching the client move through this horror, like Darth Vader watching the evil emperor killing Luke

Skywalker. Even now, after so many years, it is very hard for me to witness these events and sit there silently, but I do.

I know of only one thing to do in these endless minutes. I pray. I pray very seriously and profoundly. I pray intense prayers. I ask God to please unburden this person's soul, for this person surely has suffered enough. I pray to myself in Latin, in Slovak, the language of my ancestors, and sometimes I pray in English, but always I pray to myself. No one knows I'm praying except me. I don't know whom it helps more, me or the client, but at least I'm doing something that does not impede the process.

With Georgia, everything seemed to dissipate. She stopped crying, she stopped shivering, and her normal color came back to her face. It seemed the worst was over for now. I took the stimulators from her hands and helped her back into the chair. She asked if it was OK if she lay down on the couch.

"Of course," I said.

"I think that's about all I can do today."

"You've done plenty."

"Can I please have my water?" she asked.

I retrieved the glass of water for her and asked, "How are you doing?"

"Better," she replied. "I'm exhausted. I had forgotten about that memory. My mother choked me because I told her my dad was touching me in my privates at night. I thought she'd save me. I thought she'd make him stop, but instead she screamed and went crazy. She started slapping me and hitting me, and then she threw me outside in the cold and snow.

"If I think about it, this memory sums up my life with my parents and even my brothers. I was in no-man's-land, out in a cold desolate place where nothing and no one was safe for me. No wonder I started doing drugs. I was physically abused in the house, or going to my dad's workshop to be sexually abused. He molested me in that shop many times. I was frozen, literally and emotionally, in that memory.

"Then I started to see all the sexual abuse my father did to me as a toddler and little girl in that workshop. Those scenes were flying through my mind one after another. There were so many I could hardly bear to watch these things in my mind."

"You are courageous for hanging in there and getting through it all today," I said. "How did you get out of the cold? What made the shivering stop?"

"I went to my girlfriend's house across the street," she said. "I remember I was in my bare feet and pajamas, and they warmed me up. I remember her mom made hot chocolate for me. I loved them. I wanted to be in that family. My friend's mother was always so kind to me."

I asked her what the original upsetting memory that we had started with felt like for her right now, and she was shocked to realize that the memory of the physical altercation with her mother that had always caused her emotional distress was no longer a problem. She said, "I feel nothing when I think of that memory."

Georgia had experienced some of the most horrible

abuse from her mother and father that I have ever heard of. I am sharing just a tip of the proverbial iceberg. She marched through the stages of her passion with courage and grace.

After our work, everything began to change for her. She was no longer a person who survived each day, but instead she began to live. She began to see me less and less often. She learned to scuba dive, and she started a new career. She stated that she had never felt such happiness and content- ment. She had never thought she would experience happi- ness, because she never had in the past. She wasn't sure she would even recognize what the emotion of happiness was if she did feel it. Now she does know what it's like, and she is living a happy and fulfilled life. Suicide is no longer in her plans.

Finally, and for the first time in twenty years, she de- cided to visit her mother on Mother's Day. I do not encour- age clients to seek out their abusers. It's up to each individu- al. I do tell them that their salvation does not lie in the hands of the person who victimized them. I say, "It's within you, not out there with them."

I also give them my views on forgiveness. There is a prerequisite for being forgiven by someone. The abusers have to apologize for the harm they have done. With these perpetrators, however, it never happens. I do not remember one person ever telling me that their abuser or abusers asked for their forgiveness; not once.

After her breakthrough, Georgia had EMDR therapy sessions regularly for months. Not every session was like this, and we did not do EMDR every session. There is a need for processing and talking between such sessions. Her entire journey, ironically, took about nine months — the same as the gestational period of a fetus from conception to birth.

2

What is EMDR?

Nicole came to me because she was having frequent panic attacks. She was a middle-aged mother of three boys who were not yet in their teens. Her husband had a successful career as a software engineer. She spent her days volunteering at local schools, working for her church, and caring for her family. By most standards, she was living a wonderful life, and she said as much. I explained that I was going to interview her today to try to understand what had brought her into my office and also to try to get to know her a little better.

She immediately stopped me and said, "Before we begin, doctor, I have to ask you something, if that's OK?"

I'm not much for self-disclosure with my patients, especially one I just met a minute ago, but I agreed.

"OK," I said. "What would you like to ask me?"

"I have to know. Have you accepted Jesus Christ as your own personal savior?"

Hmmm . . . the answer to her question was, "Yes, I believe in Christ, but I'm not considered a Christian by many denominations." From my perspective, my particular religion has nothing to do with anything that I do in my office.

I did not want to get into a debate with her about whose Christianity is right or wrong.

"I will answer your question, but I will not answer any follow-up questions about my religious beliefs," I said. She agreed. "Yes, I am a Christian, although probably not a very good one."

An immediate look of relief came over her face. "Yeah, I must not be a very good Christian, either," she said. "If only I had more faith, if only I prayed hard enough, Jesus would deliver me from these panic attacks."

I hear this kind of lament quite often. Florida is a conservative state, and a number of large Christian churches are in the vicinity of my office. I have a prepared response to this kind of thinking, and I hoped it would put her mind at ease.

"Look, Nicole, if you fell, and you knew that the fall had broken your arm because the bone was protruding out of your skin, would you pray to Jesus and wait for him to fix it, or would you go to the emergency room?"

She laughed. "I would go to the emergency room, of course. I'm not crazy."

Panic attacks are often caused by something that happened to people a long time ago and predisposed them to feel anxiety. They probably do not know what it was, and they do not have to know, but it's my job to figure it out. It's what I do every day and all day. I am the doctor of emotions. Some part of a client's emotional system is malfunctioning, and I am the doctor who helps correct the malfunction. I get the system to work properly again.

Nicole seemed to accept this. "OK. I get it," she said, "But I'm still going to pray to God to take away these panic attacks."

"That's fine. I'm a fan of prayer; prayer is always a good thing," I said. "But sometimes asking God to end the panic attack is not the best prayer. When you pray, you might ask God what he is trying to tell you about yourself by giving you these panic attacks. It has been my experience that these attacks have a powerful meaning for your life."

"That sounds like a good idea," Nicole said. "But, to be honest with you, I can't imagine what the message is. These panic attacks are terrible and frightening."

"I know," I replied, "but we'll figure it out."

After we had a few sessions of ordinary talk therapy, I suggested that we try EMDR. The light bar that I use stands on one side of the room. She was not sure what to make of it, and she was not sure if her minister would allow her to do EMDR. This was not the first time I had heard that a minister, who had no idea how to treat anxiety and no idea what EMDR is or does, was the one making the decision about a client's treatment protocol.

I began to explain what EMDR is, what it does, how it works, and what she could expect to experience if she used it. I also explained why I thought it was an important method to try. It is not unusual for me to have to explain EMDR and to convince people to consider using it, so I told her what I tell everyone and what I am about to tell you.

EMDR is short for Eye Movement Desensitization and Reprocessing. It is an accelerated and adaptive model of therapy that can sometimes resolve severe problems in a few sessions.

More than twenty controlled studies, and more than four hundred additional research studies, have found EMDR to be effective in decreasing or completely eliminating symptoms related to trauma and anxiety. EMDR is one of the most researched therapies.

EMDR is used and endorsed by the U.S. Department of Veterans Affairs as the therapy of choice for soldiers returning from Iraq and Afghanistan with post-traumatic stress disorder. This organization does not make such recommendations unless the treatment is heavily researched and shows significant positive results.

It seems as if EMDR is one of the best-kept secrets in the world. Despite its amazing healing properties to resolve emotional distress, it is not well known or understood by the public. In fact, only a handful of my patients have ever heard of it.

EMDR was discovered in 1987 by Francine Shapiro, a California psychology student, who was told the traumatic news that she had breast cancer. She was extremely upset by this news, as you might imagine. She was a young woman in 1987, with her entire life in front of her. The word cancer is a frightening word to hear from your doctor today, but in 1987, it was often a death sentence.

Ms. Shapiro often recounts the story of her discovery in conferences and in her books. She stated that she went for a walk in the park. She said that she had been reading about eye movements as a way to reduce emotional distress, as she began moving her eyes back and forth. After she did this for some minutes, she noticed that when she tried to think of the upsetting thoughts, she was less upset about them.

She thought that this eye-movement process she'd just stumbled upon might be an interesting thing to study under scientific methods to determine if it had some promise. The study was the first of many.[7]

Thankfully, she recovered from cancer, and she developed EMDR into one of the most powerful therapies in the world today. More than two million people have been treated with EMDR, and thousands of mental health professionals are trained in EMDR, with more being trained every day. This is a potent therapeutic tool that has provided extraordinary results for many problems.

There are a number of distinctions between EMDR and other traditional forms of therapy. EMDR is extremely effective and efficient. In other words, it works very fast. Also, there have been studies where the subjects were re-interviewed five, ten, and even fifteen years later to determine if the effects remained in place, and they did.

EMDR seems to create a permanent fix. It is a process of actually stimulating the clients' own brain and central nervous systems to resolve distressing events that may have occurred years ago. Once they are resolved, the clients begin to function at a much higher level.

If these clients are willing to do comprehensive EMDR work, they will move through the six stages of transformation that will be presented in this book. They will become their most authentic and true selves, no longer encumbered by trying to be what other people want them to be, or afraid to try to be who they want to be because someone told them long ago that they're just not good enough.

EMDR creates for them a clear view of their own reality, which becomes free of emotional problems from the past. Our histories often cloud and confuse our realities. Unfortunately, these emotional realities are often driven by unconscious machinery that was created years ago, but that still runs our lives without our being aware of it.

Nicole asked, "How can EMDR help me, if I do not know what causes these panic attacks?"

"That is one of the beautiful things about the EMDR process," I said. "It seeks and destroys the connected events in people's lives that are causing trouble for them in the present. EMDR finds the answer."

One of my EMDR trainers often said to me, "Remember, Andy, *it's never about now.*" Clients don't usually buy into the "it's about your childhood" idea, but the problems *are* almost always about the past.

The more I do this work, the more I know this to be true. Clients will come in and tell me they overreacted to something someone said or did to them. They know they overreacted, but they were unable to control themselves for some reason.

Many models of psychotherapy have taught that problems in the present are about things that happened in the past. We only need look at veterans with flashbacks. The war may have been over for decades, but their trauma can be triggered by something that makes them feel as if they are back in a war zone of their past.

EMDR is able to resolve these old memories and bring people to an internal sense of peace and contentment, sometimes for the first time in their lives. This place of contentment gives people a clear view of themselves. It truly allows them to be their most authentic selves, selves that they understand and accept.

EMDR does not simply treat clients; it heals and often transforms them permanently. My job is to resolve anxiety, depression, and traumatic issues, and when the client does comprehensive transforming work, I am in my element, and they have come to the right place.

Transformative work changes clients into the people they are supposed to be. EMDR does this by dismantling their core negative beliefs, such as, "I'm not good enough," "I don't matter," "I'm to blame" or whatever it happens to be. These are more than words; they are the driving forces in peoples' lives that lead them down the wrong path.

When this work is finished, their hearts, souls, minds and bodies are in alignment. Everything is as it should be, and they can get on with their life's work.

"How do we start?" Nicole inquired.

"I'm glad you asked. We start with a timeline of distressing events."

She asked, "What do you mean?"

"Well, it doesn't have to be on a line, and it doesn't have to be chronological," I said. "It's a list of events that, when you think about them, you feel something. The EMDR community calls it a 'trauma timeline,' but that's too harsh. People will often say, 'I've never had a trauma,' or they will minimize a trauma and not put it on their list, so I like to say 'distressing events.'

"Nicole, I like to say 'timeline' because I want you to recall some of the earliest upsetting moments you can recall, even if you were very small, because when someone yells at a child, that child does not have the intellectual power to protect herself. She just feels very upset and does not know what to do other than cry. A lot of the time, these moments have lifelong impacts on the way we behave and feel about ourselves and our world."

Nicole said: "I can think of one or two things right off the bat. When I was a little girl, still in diapers, my grandpa molested me, and I was raped in college, and three years ago my husband gambled my inheritance away after my father passed on. Is that what you mean, that kind of stuff?"

"Yes," I said, and I went on:

"There's another thing. I want you to think about less traumatic events as well as the worst ones. Here's why. Let me share a part of my timeline. Yes, I have an EMDR therapist, and I, too, have used EMDR to clear out the clutter in my psyche. My first memory was of first grade.

"I loved school. I loved my friends. I loved my teacher. I loved everything about it. Nevertheless, one day when we were doing some assignment, I used crayons rather than a pencil because I had misunderstood the instructions. When the teacher saw this, she violently yanked me out of my chair and smacked me on my behind a few times. I remember almost wetting myself. No one had ever laid a hand on me before. I had wonderful parents who never resorted to violence of any kind.

"That moment doesn't bother me now, but at that moment my entire view of my little world changed. After that moment, nothing was ever the same again. My core belief was born on that day.

"You see, I realized a truth about the world. Teachers are not always nice; in fact, they can be very dangerous. I thought I was doing well in school, a good student, but apparently I was a bad student, because in a class of forty kids I was the only one who was ever singled out, yelled at, and hit. So although I never admitted my core belief to myself, it was implied in my thinking, feeling, and behavior.

"I learned to make sure I never made a mistake again. I learned to be afraid to make any kind of mark on my paper unless I had watched at least one other person in my class put down a similar mark. I learned to be quiet and to fly under the radar. I learned to do whatever I had to do to make sure that never happened again.

"You see, I did not have the intellectual understanding to say, 'Oh, the poor old lady probably just had a fight with her husband last night,' and forget about the whole thing.

"It's not my teacher's fault that we, as humans, are designed to attract trouble, but we are. Sometimes clients will put something on their list that might seem to be a rather neutral event, and yet they are in tears when they talk of it. When I hear and see their anguish, I realize there is no way to get through life without having to struggle through a negative or irrational belief about yourself.

"That is why I want you to think about your earliest up-setting memories."

"That sounds fine, doc," Nicole said, "But I already know my core belief; you already said it. I think I have more than one."

"Me, too," I said. "What are they?"

" 'I don't matter' is probably the big one," she said, "then 'I'm not good enough,' and 'I'm to blame.' 'I'm to blame' is a big one, too. When I was growing up, I was blamed for everything. My brother was always in trouble, and my parents would baby him and make excuses for him, but me, I got blamed for everything, even if the weather was bad."

She was angry, and she cried as she told me this. When I identify people's core beliefs, they are often brought to tears. They may have felt these beliefs and lived them but never uttered those words to themselves. Once the words are said to them, they know that this is their truth. This has been their truth for a long time, and it is a wrong and unjust truth that must change.

They have just been invited to their crucifixion, the crucifixion of this old destructive way, and I am the executioner, but also the midwife who will bring their new selves to life, to the birth of the new adaptive way.

Nicole would move out of the world of "I don't matter" to the world of "I do matter." It sounded simple, but she was in for one of the biggest struggles of her life. She was about to encounter her soul and dismantle part of it.

When she came back with her timeline, it looked

something like this:

> Grandpa
> Susie didn't want to be friends anymore
> Dad's violence (Vietnam Vet, PTSD, and Alcohol)
> Turning over the kitchen table in a rage
> Blamed for everything including the weather
> College rape
> Depression and quit college
> Abortion and miscarriage
> Dad's death
> Money gone

From this timeline, I determined her core beliefs. She had a few — from the rape, quitting college (because of the rape), abortion (caused by the rape), miscarriage, Susie no longer being a friend, and grandpa molesting her.

It is common for victims of abuse as children to blame themselves as adults. Intellectually, Nicole was completely aware of the fact that these events had not been her fault, but emotionally she felt they had been. EMDR aligned her heart with what her head knew to be true. The intellect cannot heal these wounds, but we began to heal them with EMDR.

With Nicole, we began one session with her father yelling at her because it was raining and he had just washed his car. She needed an image, a photograph in her mind of an event, as a place to start. Once she had this picture, which was of the rage on her father's face that she had witnessed thousands of times, then she could add the core belief. For her, it was, as we had discussed, "I'm to blame."

She was sitting about three feet from the light bar in my office, a bar about thirty inches long and four feet from the ground. A row of blue lights moved back and forth on the bar at a pretty fast clip.

A client can also wear headphones that beep alternately, synchronized with the movement of the lights. If the lights are moving to the right, the right headphone will beep, and vice versa. Also, a client can hold in her hands small paddles that vibrate as the lights move and the headphones beep. A client may use any combination of these modes of stimulation: all three of them, two, or just one.

Nicole chose the lights and paddles and did not want the headphones, which was fine.

I said to her: "It is important to keep your head still and only move your eyes to track the lights back and forth. The bi-lateral stimulation occurs when your pupils move from one corner of your eye socket to the other side. OK?"

She understood and agreed.

In the first EMDR treatment session, I always establish a "safe place" with my client, an image in the client's mind's eye of a calming place, perhaps the beach, or a favorite chair at home. I had done this with Nicole, so I said: "Remember, you can stop any time, and you can use your safe place to calm down if you feel the need to stop. You're the boss. You're in control. I'm here just to keep you safe and help move the process along."

She said that she understood.

Finally, I said: "Remember, this is not going to be like last time. The safe place was slow and relaxing. This session will be fast and stimulating. Your job is not to try and make something happen, nor are you to prevent anything from happening. You are a passive vessel allowing whatever comes up to manifest itself in here. Do not push anything down. If you feel like crying, cry. If you feeling like being angry, be angry. If your body starts to feel something, just let it feel it.

"It's best not to talk. At some point, I am going to ask you this simple question, 'What are you noticing?' I do not need a review of the last two or three minutes, but I want to know what the most prominent thing is that you are aware of at that particular moment."

Finally, I said: "Anything that comes up for you in here stays in here with me when you leave, but if you push it down and repress it, you get to take it back home with you. Do you understand? Are you ready?"

"As ready as I'll ever be," she said. "Let's get started."

I hit the remote "Start" button, and she was off.

For EMDR to work best, we like the thought to be as general as possible. In that way, EMDR moves though the client's past in a broad way to seek and destroy any connected memory about this belief. For example, we would never use a thought like, "I'm to blame for the weather." That limits the EMDR process only to events related to the weather. If we just keep it as "I'm to blame," the psyche can move though any moment in Nicole's life when she was driven by this thought, not just those moments caused by her father and his displeasure with the weather.

EMDR assists people to function better by dismantling their core negative beliefs. EMDR removes blocks that prevent us from performing optimally. We all carry baggage, easily identified by our negative blocking beliefs. These beliefs are usually the source of problems, and EMDR removes these kinds of beliefs permanently.

Once treated, Nicole never again had her sense of "I'm to blame." When she truly experienced the reality, when she could say to herself and believe in every cell of her being that "I didn't do anything wrong," her entire life completely changed.

She agreed that I was truly her emotional doctor who had healed her broken emotions, but she did not stop crediting Christ. "Jesus sent me to you so you can help me understand and accept all the terrible things that happened to me," she said. "I never thought about them or accepted them. I'd just hide from those terrible memories."

I never know what to say when people say these things to me. It is a great compliment and, perhaps, not a bad way to spend a day, being an instrument of God to heal those who are in trouble. Me an instrument of God? That's for priests and ministers. I just do what I do, what I love to do, and what I have some skill in doing. It's nice when things work out and people find contentment because of our work together.

If people only knew how little I do in EMDR sessions! EMDR and the client do all the work. I'm just there watching, making sure the client is safely processing what needs to be metabolized in their psyche. My role is like that of a guide assisting them on this inner journey.

During the processing of EMDR there is little talking, with only sparse comments or questions from me. Once the mindful state of processing is in motion, once the portal to the collective unconscious is accessed, I want to keep it open, so that my access to what is going on can be very quick.

Nicole finished her work with me. She gave me a hug at the last session and said: "Andrew, these past months you have been a true companion of mine in Christ, perhaps more than anyone in my life. The ironic thing is that we never talked about Jesus, but I felt him here in many of these sessions. I will never forget what I learned here and what you did for me. Thank you."

"You're quite welcome, but, Nicole, you did all the heavy lifting on this journey," I said. "It was a pleasure working with someone so dedicated and brave in this process."

She was right about God being around for some of her sessions. Some of them were electric. She would respond to my standard query, "What are you noticing?" with insight and clarity that would make the hairs on my arm stand up.

Her insights were not from her ego or intellect; they were from some wiser self. Call it the collective unconscious, call it your higher self, or call it the voice of God. I do not care what you call it, but whatever it is, it does not exist in conversation. It only exists in the silence of the client's mind.

In one dramatic session, she figured it out. She saw the connection.

When I first asked her where she had her panic attacks, she said: "Anywhere. They come out of the blue, and for no reason. It seems so unfair and so unjust. It is ridiculous. I could see if there was a reason. You know, like if I was stuck in an elevator, or in a big crowd, or in the middle of a row in a crowded movie theater. But it happens anywhere, at any time, and for no logical reason."

During this emotional EMDR session, she began to weep when I asked her, "What are you noticing?"

"It's out of the blue!"

"What's out of the blue?" I asked.

She said: "That's it, doc. It comes out of the blue. My father's rage came out of the blue, for no reason, so unfair, so unjust. I was helpless and afraid in his world, just like in these panic attacks. These panic attacks are treating me just like my father, and I am done with them both."

"OK, Nicole, go with that. Go with 'out of the blue.' "

She did, and we continued the process. She was healed of her panic attacks that day, and she never had another.

In that session, she began by hating her father, allowing herself to feel her rage for the first time. Intense rage showed on her face as she pressed against the vibrating paddles in her hand until her knuckles turned white.

She hated her panic attacks. She hated everything she had ever blamed herself for and everyone who had made her feel blame for things she had not done. After about twenty minutes, her feelings shifted, as they always do, and her intense rage gave way to a calm, peaceful state.

Then she said: "My dad had a rough life. He got a raw deal in Vietnam. He never recovered from it. I can let it go; I can let what he did to me go. It is long overdue. I can be at peace with him. I feel peace toward him. I never, ever felt peace toward him. I would shudder at the word 'dad.' I cannot believe I'm saying this and feeling like it is true. How can this be happening?"

"I don't really know how," I said. "I just know that it is happening, and it is not going to change back." She was mystified, exhilarated, and exhausted.

I thought back to what she had said about her father. She had said that his rage would come "out of the blue and for no reason." She was right! Her father and her panic attacks had treated her in exactly the same way. My supervisor had been right, too: "It's never about now."

3

A New Map of the Soul

In the illustration on the following page, you will see the map of the soul or, if you prefer, the map of the human psyche. At one end of the map is our birth. On the opposite end is the rebirth. We are exposed to the negative self-beliefs early in life. I have had some clients say they felt trauma in the womb, so it can all start very early. Some common beliefs are on the left-hand side of the diagram, such as I'm not good enough, I'm to blame, etc. These negative beliefs are established in these early years and then, when crisis of some kind strikes, we begin to try and resolve these issues. Of course, some of us remain completely in the dark about these issues. As I have said, and will continue to say, much of my time early on as I work with clients is to convince them that their childhood is affecting their present lives.

I shared the story of Nicole so you can understand the impact our early life has on each one of us throughout the life span, unless we get an understanding of our past so we can limit its impact on the future.

I'm reminded of an eighty-five-year-old retired Irish priest who came to see me after retirement to finally come to terms with his abusive mother. He did a lot of work with

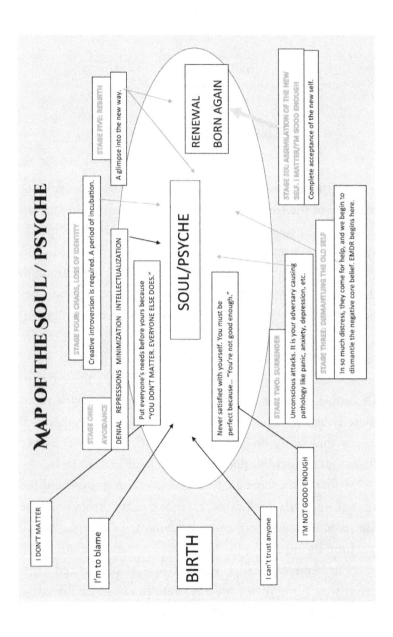

MAP OF THE SOUL / PSYCHE

STAGE ONE: AVOIDANCE

DENIAL   REPRESSIONS   MINIMIZATION   INTELLECTUALIZATION

Put everyone's needs before yours because "YOU DON'T MATTER. EVERYONE ELSE DOES."

STAGE FOUR: CHAOS, LOSS OF IDENTITY

Creative introversion is required. A period of incubation.

STAGE FIVE: REBIRTH

A glimpse into the new way.

STAGE SIX: ASSIMILATION OF THE NEW SELF. I MATTER/I'M GOOD ENOUGH

Complete acceptance of the new self.

RENEWAL
BORN AGAIN

SOUL/PSYCHE

Never satisfied with yourself. You must be perfect because... "You're not good enough."

STAGE TWO: SURRENDER

Unconscious attacks. It is your adversary causing pathology like panic, anxiety, depression, etc.

STAGE THREE: DISMANTLING THE OLD SELF

In so much distress, they come for help, and we begin to dismantle the negative core belief. EMDR begins here.

I DON'T MATTER

I'm to blame

BIRTH

I can't trust anyone

I'M NOT GOOD ENOUGH

me and passed away shortly after we had finished our work together. Emotional wounds do not submit to chronological time.

The common negative core beliefs on the left-hand side of the map precede the work and are not part of the six stages. Accumulating issues occurs long before the work starts. The various stages are marked with bold gray letters linked to a brief descriptor of what occurs in each stage. This book will expand on this map. Stage one is avoidance, which can last a very long time. Sometimes there is denial that there are any issues to resolve at all. This also usually happens outside of my office.

Stage two on the map is a surrendering. Here the client is willing to get help, usually because there is some type of emotional distress in the person's life. Stage three is the work of dismantling the negative core belief and causing the emotional distress to dissipate. In my work, this is the beginning of the EMDR work. Stage four is a period of confusion. Sometimes the person feels a loss of identity because they are free of their past. This is no small thing, and usually a new set of problems has to be addressed. Stage five is the rebirth and the beginning of the acceptance of the new way. Stage six is the final stage, when the new way is completely accepted and the person has a new sense of calm.

This is the map we are about to follow in the next chapters. We will discuss the number of ways the negative belief comes to exist in a person's life. We will discuss how this belief is dismantled and profoundly changes the client. We will discuss each stage and compare it to its Christian counterpart, as this psychological process has a direct parallel to a true Christian journey. We will interpret some of Christ's most misunderstood words through the lens of the true death and resurrection journey on the human psyche. Finally, we will discuss tools and skills that will expedite this process, such as journaling, dream work, and the powerful use of the imagination.

Let's begin by examining and understanding where the process all begins, and that is the insidious nature and the birth of the negative core belief.

I should mention that this process is not linear. It is not logical. One can be in three separate stages at the same time. The book is also not linear. One has to read the entire book and let it metabolize. I did my best to present the stages in order, but when using examples that use symbols, signs and emotion rather than intellect, it is difficult, so I let the material flow as it was experienced. This structure was not by design as much as this is the way it is.

4

Birth of Trouble:
The Insidious Nature
of the Negative Core Belief

Let's take a closer look at just how powerful a negative core belief is and how much damage it can do in a person's life. Negative core beliefs are identified by simple statements like, "I don't matter," or "I'm not good enough." These few simple words represent a person's endless years of struggle filled with wrong turns and bad decisions. They represent a fixed template that controls behavior out of our awareness. This template is set very early in life, even in the womb, and as time goes on, it becomes more rigid and more powerful.

Negative beliefs before she could walk or talk

Margaret was the younger sibling of a family where males were revered and women, not so much. She was the second female born to her family. When she was born, the family story goes that when her father learned of her gender he wept, punched a hole in his kitchen wall and fell to the floor in tears. This was before he ever saw her. She insisted that he came to love her and she adored her father and he adored his family. This story, however, begins the negative core belief for Margaret. This story was no secret, and it was told often at family gatherings.

This new baby was physically abused by her older sibling, only two years her senior, to the extent that she had to be sent away to live with relatives to learn how to walk because the older sibling would always push her down. The parents did little to intervene except to send her away. Her negative core beliefs were born before she could even talk. She was not good enough, she did not matter, and she was most certainly a disappointment, all before she could walk or talk.

She learned very early on that it was safest to be alone. Alone was where she loved to be, and she sought out solitude her entire life. She was quiet and invisible in her family; that was safest. When she was five, she made up a nursery rhyme that she often sang to her favorite baby doll, and she sang it to me some fifty years later:

> Beautiful girl
> Happy and married,
> all by herself.
> Oh yes, beautiful girl,
> happy and married
> all by herself.

When I met her she was in her fifties and had children whom she described as great kids. She was married to a wealthy Wall Street man who lived most of every month in New York City; he would come home to visit for eight or nine days a month. She created the exact life that her little nursery rhyme said she would become. Happy, married, and alone; she was married all by herself.

Although being alone was a good place for her as a child, it does not work out so well when you are an adult and married. Marriage is supposed to be a relationship, an intimate relationship; it is not something that should be done alone. In the end, the template was set, and its power was completely out of her awareness, as it is with all of us. We re-create what we know, not what is best for us. This template must be recognized and dismantled. This is the work I do.

This client was reluctant to blame her past history on her present circumstance until she recalled the little song she made up as a child and realized she was living that song. That was a difficult session, truly a soul-shaking moment, kind of like Dorothy — one minute you're in Kansas, and the next minute you're in Oz. It is often a hard thing to accept that the life you have been living is not the life you are supposed to be living.

She later shifted to the adaptive positive core belief. She made this positive and permanent shift. She felt good enough. She did not feel like a disappointment or that she was to blame for things that were not her fault. She was a new and empowered woman shaking up a family system that needed to change, and it did.

I remember the day she made the shift to the positive

thought in the midst of an EMDR session. I asked, "What are you noticing?"

She responded, "I'm seeing a large field of pink petunias." I love to hear an image, because the soul is shouting something wonderful even though it seems more like a whisper or even nonsense. I love nonsense in the session. I'll discuss this further later.

I said, "OK, go with that."

Then she started to get tearful, so I waited a bit and asked again, "What are you noticing?"

She said: "My grandmother called me her little petunia. I spent a lot of time alone with her. She loved me. I mattered to her." That was it. That was the beginning of the adaptive shift to her authentic self. She was moving to stage five and six. She recalled many memories that reminded her that she did indeed matter.

Her story was much like that of Nicole, who discovered it was all about her father and his treatment of her as a child and a young adult. The core belief is where it all begins, and then, after years of struggle, we realize something is wrong, something isn't working, and hopefully one seeks out help to become who we are meant to truly be.

'I can't handle this' people

I had a client who was a very successful businessman, and he had been an excellent scholar and athlete in high school. He had done it all.

You see, home was dangerous. His father and mother

were both raging alcoholics. He joined every club, played every sport, and studied until the library was closed. He could sense when a fight was about to break out, and he'd be gone in a flash.

He had the belief, "I can't handle this." All of his successes and high praise from many other adults had let him know that he mattered, but once his parents started fighting, he couldn't handle it and left the house.

He had learned that any sign of emotion meant it was time to leave. This was adaptive as a young man growing up. He had won awards, earned a scholarship, and avoided fights with his parents. Running at any expression of emotion had been a good and safe way to live. It served him well.

Later, when he was a grown man with a wife and daughter, a tragedy struck. His twenty-year-old daughter was diagnosed with stage four cancer. His wife was an emotional wreck, as you might imagine, because she was terrified about her daughter's condition. The daughter was afraid but brave, and my client, well, he did what he always did during highly emotional situations — he bolted. He took a two-year job in Japan, leaving his wife to care for their daughter alone in the States. He just did what he always had done in similar emotional situations. Everything always worked out for him when he bolted during high emotion. He remained safe. He survived. He even got awards for it, so his emotional engine went into gear and did the thing he knew how to do: Run.

The template was set long ago, and no amount of willpower could change his behavior. He was no match for the powerful emotional machinery that he had been building his entire life. It was nuclear, and you cannot talk logically to nuclear emotion power. It won't work.

This couple survived, however, and so did their daughter. My client came to understand why he did what he did when his family needed him most. With the help of EMDR and an understanding wife, he changed. The most important factor was that he wanted to change, when he realized he needed to stop running. "I can't handle this" became "I can handle this."

Emotions, when ignored, create havoc with our lives. The template is like gravity. It is not a theory, it is a law, and we as humans treat it as if it doesn't exist because we can't see it. This emotional template that we all have, this emotional machinery that we have been building our entire lives, will cause our world to be what it always has been. This, of course, is never what it is meant to be.

No one could talk my client out of his decision to go to Japan. The process was not logical. If it had been a logical problem, he would have figured it out, because he was a very smart man. It was an emotional equation, and he, like most all of us in this country, have absolutely no understanding of how our emotions work and how powerful they are when left to their own devices.

So you can see that core negative beliefs are no small thing. Some other popular core beliefs that people struggle with are "I'm not good enough," "I can't trust," "I'm not in control" and "I should have done something." These are not just sentences, but rather symbolic representations of the devastation caused by refusing to look inward in search of the authentic self.

The negative core belief that initially creates adaptive behaviors when we are young must change as an adult. The client who sought to be alone was making a very adaptive and smart decision as a child. It kept her safe. The problem: No one tells us when to let go of the old behavior, so we keep on doing what we have always done, just like my businessman client who went off to Japan and my female client who was married all by herself.

The many faces of *I don't matter*

Let's examine a few other ways that the "I don't matter" cognition can be created. Frequently, children of one or more alcoholic parents learn early on that alcohol mattered but they did not.

Alcoholics behave in a way that teaches their children that they do not matter. Only alcohol matters. The children learn this because the alcoholic father does not attend their soccer games, awards ceremonies, or anything else that children would like their fathers to support. The father chooses instead to drink with his friends until he's drunk, comes home to eat, and passes out or goes into a rage over some trivial issue.

It can be the same for ambitious parents whose job matters more than anything. The child learns the same thing. Mom or dad can't attend this activity or that activity because they are busy working late or out of town. Or this belief can grow out of having simply selfish parents who probably should never have had children.

Children of such parents have this core belief that drives their adult lives. Unfortunately, they are completely unaware of this belief, much like my client who went to Japan. "I don't matter" is a devastating way to think of oneself. They live under the reign of "you don't matter" dictators, directing their every move, without even being aware of it.

When people have this core belief, they engage the world as a doormat. They expect the world to treat them poorly, as if they don't matter, because that's how it's always been. They find friends who will treat them like doormats. They marry spouses who are selfish and perpetuate the world of "I don't matter" for them.

I once had a female client who worked long hours, sometimes six days a week. Why? She would always work overtime if she was asked, because everyone else's needs were more important than hers. "Oh, Suzy had a dinner party with her husband or John had to take his son to a basketball game." So she was always stuck working because nothing she had to do mattered as much as a fellow employee's needs.

She told me during one session that she had to go to Tallahassee on Saturday and return Sunday to be at work early on Monday because her mother and father needed help cleaning their garage.

"That's the purpose of the six-hour drive, to help them clean their garage?" I asked.

"Yes, and I don't want to go. I've been working. I just

worked twelve days in a row. I am exhausted."

"Isn't there anyone between here and Tallahassee you could pay to do that?"

"I could never say no to my parents," she replied.

Fortunately, EMDR opened her eyes to these frequent and ridiculous requests. She did not go to help clean out the garage. She learned to say no to her parents and to her fellow workers. She was surprised that the world did not end, that no one hated her, and no one thought she was selfish. Her life became more peaceful as she started to think about her own needs first, for the first time in her life.

اللہ

Clients like these never felt that they deserved anything. As adults, they didn't even know what their needs or wants were. They never even pondered a thought that considers their needs and desires. Many clients live this kind of life. One client did not know if she liked ketchup or not. "My dad put mustard on my hotdog and told me to eat it, so that's what I did and still do," she said.

"Did you ever try ketchup?" I asked.

She replied: "No. My dad always told me to eat my hotdog with mustard, so that's what I do."

"But your dad died eight years ago," I said.

She knew what I was getting at, and she was silent. Finally, she said, "Maybe I should try it."

This was a small beginning, which led to her becoming her own woman. As long as she was doing what people wanted her to do and never asking the question, "What do I want?" she slowly became depressed and eventually emotionally crushed. Our soul does not want others to determine our life's path. Each one of us has to determine how to fulfill our life — no one else can or should do that for us. Otherwise, you will eventually be met with an attack from within.

All of us are in danger that the unconscious will attack at some point and create emotional distress, so that we can get on with our truth. Our life's work is where our God-given talents will be nurtured and grow.

A female client entered my office and said: "Doc, I married three abusive alcoholics in fifteen years. I do not know what is wrong with me, but I do not want to marry another."

What brought her into my office is a rather amusing story, and it demonstrates the unconscious power that this "I don't matter" belief represents. Not that three bad marriages aren't evidence enough, but this case demonstrates the even greater and mysterious nature of our unconscious, a nature that we cannot manage without help.

She told the story:

"I swore I was never going to date an alcoholic or even a man who drinks again. I decided to go to a singles dance for those over forty-five years old. You know, it was for adult singles. This dance was at my church. There was not a drop of alcohol within five miles of this place.

"I met a man I really liked. We talked the night away. The night flew by. I couldn't believe it was time to leave. I couldn't wait to see him again. We arranged a date for the next weekend. He chose a really nice restaurant, so I was looking forward to a wonderful evening. Unfortunately, that was not to be. This guy was tanked before we finished our appetizers. How is this possible? What is wrong with me? In a room full of Christian men, with no alcohol in sight, I go right to the raging alcoholic in the room!"

The answer was not hard to figure out. Her father was an alcoholic. Alcohol mattered in her childhood. She didn't. Dad went to the bar to drink, and that's about all she knew about him. So she learned how to "not matter."

She was a well-educated and successful woman. As I said, and will continue to say, if the problem could be solved intellectually, she would have figured it out, but it was not a thinking thing.

EMDR treatment dismantled the "I don't matter" machinery for my client. She began to insist on being valued and treated with the respect she deserved. She could say the words, "I matter" and believe this statement in every cell in her body. She met a good man who cared for her and loved her. He did not drink.

Once we dismantle the negative core belief, some behavior training is needed to help with assertiveness. A person who never says "no" has to learn how to say it. When someone in a family has no value other than serving the other members and now insists on having his or her needs met and valued, there is usually trouble. Families do not like to deal with members changing roles.

Clients perpetuate the "I don't matter" belief in many

ways. One client who had this core belief was married in her twenties to an extremely violent, controlling, and abusive man, from whom she had to seek shelter.

I met her when she was in her forties. She was complaining about her second husband, who was rather unemotional and docile. She was not going to marry another violent man, so she had chosen his opposite.

The ironic part of this story is that he, also, treated her as if she did not matter. She would ask him to do something, he would agree to do it for her, and then he would not do it. Both of these men, who seemed so different from each other, perpetuated her core belief, "I don't matter." After our work together, she divorced the second man.

I warn people about these kinds of results. Once a core belief shifts with EMDR, it shifts permanently. One cannot go back to the world of "ignorance is bliss." Friends and family have to adjust, or they may be abandoned by the client who has had EMDR treatment.

I know we think that we choose our careers, but I will tell you about the nurses I have treated. Many of them have had "I don't matter" core beliefs. It was as if they had all had the same parents. Many, not all, had a story that went like this:

"I was the oldest when my little brother was born. I was six years old, and he was my responsibility. I would have to feed him, bathe him and put him to bed. I was like his mother. My parents were always out or drunk."

I was shocked when I first heard this tale, but after hearing more of the traumatic experiences my clients had endured, it seemed rather tame. They had learned at a young age how to take care of people. Often they would feel responsible for a parent's feelings, thinking that they did something wrong to cause mom to cry or that they caused their parents' divorce.

The bottom line is that my clients had not mattered, and they had learned how to care for another person at a very young age, so as adults they had continued to care for others and to put the needs of others before themselves. What better way to perpetuate your family's pathology and your negative core belief than continuing to do what you've always done, by becoming a nurse? Don't get me wrong: All nurses do not have this story, but many that I have treated over the years do.

Before I do EMDR with them, I warn them that they may not want to proceed with this treatment, because at the end of the process, they may hate being nurses.

At times I had misgivings about doing EMDR, because of the dramatic changes that it created. For example, it was not easy for me to watch people end relationships with friends and family, even though these relationships were toxic and often abusive. Once a person's core belief shifts from "I don't matter" to "I do matter," they cannot endure being treated like they don't matter. This change confuses families and friends because they have always treated the client poorly and he or she never complained before. Everything changes internally, which causes external changes in the world that must be navigated and managed.

This transformation exemplifies the move from stage

four to five. The rebirth is awkward. The client does not know how to matter, how to deserve, how to ask for what she wants. This is a born-again move: "You must be as a little child to enter the kingdom of heaven." The person, no matter what age, feels like a little child with a completely different view of the world. She feels unsure, but there is an inner sense of knowing this is right and it must be figured out and mastered, and it is, in relatively short order.

Two additional sayings of Jesus helped me to accept the powerful changes that I was facilitating. I never really understood these sayings until I started doing EMDR work and seeing its results. They now made sense to me.

The first quote:

> Do not suppose I have come to bring peace to the
> earth: it is not peace I have come to bring, but a sword.[8]

And:

> For I have come to set a man against his father, a
> daughter against her mother, a daughter-in-law against
> her mother-in-law. Man's enemies will be those of his
> own household.[9]

John Sanford writes in *The Kingdom Within*: "It may seem strange that Jesus should point to the member of one's own family as 'enemies.' It is precisely because there is so much love, and tribal loyalty, that one's own family can be an 'enemy' to the kingdom of God."

He continues, "Often when an identification exists with

our families which is thwarting our individuality *there must be a breaking away from them psychologically* [italics mine]. There is a need to differentiate psychologically in order that we may become free and individual."[10]

I would add a husband against his wife, or vice-versa. Often, people who do not matter marry someone who treats them like they do not matter. Once we finish EMDR, it is hard to go back into the world of "I don't matter"; in fact, it is impossible. Once a person realizes they have value, should have their own dreams, and should be cared for by others as much as they care for others, they insist on being valued. This initially feels like selfishness to them, but they soon understand that it is not selfishness; it is healthy.

One of my client's dreams exemplifies this struggle to separate from our parents if they are using their influence to keep us under their control and/or keeping us from our true purpose, from being who we really are supposed to be. She shared this dream:

"I am a physician. A couple brings in their newborn child, which is in the examination room. They greet me before we go in and say, 'She has a sore on her mouth and we just noticed it.' She walks in and looks at the baby and is horrified to see a massive grotesque sore over half the baby's face that had to take weeks or even months to grow. I thought, 'I need to get this baby away from these parents quietly, but immediately.' "

My client in this dream is both the physician and the baby. She is in stage five moving to six but is reminded that she is not finished. There is a danger that the baby can die if she does not keep the parents away from this baby, who represents the possibility of the rebirth, the transformed self.

She has been reborn, like a child ready to enter the kingdom of heaven. She does, however, have to separate from her parents' influence; otherwise, this transformation will not survive. This dream exemplified her journey, and she has made great strides in moving away from the influence of her family. She has started to make significant healthy changes for herself and her immediate family, unencumbered by trying to please her parents.

EMDR creates the opportunity to create the authentic self. People toss this word "authentic" around, but the changes are so very dramatic, and the healing so profound with EMDR, that I am confident it moves people closer to the "self" God wants them to be and to not be concerned about the man or woman their mother or father or brother or spouse or boss or sister wants them to be. They become content in their own skin. They become peaceful and content within. They become unaffected by what others think of them because they know they are doing the best that they can. Validation from the outside is nice but not necessary. This creates a powerful sense of okayness and an incredible internal peacefulness.

I tell my clients that EMDR provides the freedom to make the right decision. It does not turn you into a selfish person. You will be a person who can decide, *yes, I will go,* or *no, I will not go.* It changes the compulsion to tell yourself, "I must go," to a calmer, "Let me think about how I feel and decide what I prefer to do or not do."

There are conditions and limitations for the "doing" in the religion, but this fact seems to get lost and confused with "I don't matter" people or "I'm not good enough" people. Do unto others as you would have them do unto you, or love your neighbor as yourself. These sayings do not mean or say, "Always do what anyone asks of you at any time no matter what." Yet this is how people often behave.

"Do unto others as you would have them do unto you" means you can and should question whether to do something for someone or not. If you would never ask a person for such a favor, then it is likely that you should say no. If your neighbor says, "Hey, paint my house, please," you would not do it, because you would never ask such a thing of your neighbor. There are limits to these sayings, but sometimes it feels less scary to paint the neighbor's house than to simply say the simple word, no.

Jesus said, "Do not throw pearls before swine." What are your pearls? Your time is a pearl, perhaps the most important pearl. Your energy is a pearl. Your love is a pearl. Your respect is a pearl. Your money is a pearl.

Some people will take the last drop of blood you have. It's not their job to protect your pearls. It is your job. The "I don't matter" people have no idea how to protect theirs, but after EMDR and some behavioral training, they find themselves on the path that they were always meant to be on, the path of knowing when to say no, and the path of understanding what they need and deserve. They can now seek to fulfill their needs and get on with THEIR authentic journey.

So who should take this journey? Every single one of us

should, because no one gets out of childhood without a negative core belief that is causing trouble. If you say to yourself, "Not me," I say: "Exactly. You, my friend, are in stage one, avoidance."

Welcome to the journey, because this book is your invitation to make this journey for yourself. You might put a notebook by your bed and write your dreams down tonight. You will dream, if you let your unconscious know you want a relationship with it. Placing a pen and pad by your bed is an invitation to open a portal to your greatest ally, your unconscious, or, if you dare to say so, to God.

Morton Kelsey wrote a book titled, *Dreams: A Way of Listening to God.* John Sanford wrote a book titled, *Dreams: God's Forgotten Language.* I recommend both of these to you. They are easy to read and understand, and they will go further in making the point of just how important working with our dreams is in this modern digital world.

5

Birth of the Six-Stage Model

The last chapter described how troubles begin for us all. The rest of the book is about what to do about it.

Let's go back to Nicole for a moment. I know, some of you are probably wondering, what did the minister say to Nicole? What did he think about EMDR? Did he give his blessing to Nicole and EMDR, or did she simply defy him?

I told you her story to tell this story. This is where it all began. It began out of a great success that surprisingly turned into a failure that had to be worked out and understood.

Barbara survived one of the worst cases of PTSD (post-traumatic stress disorder) I ever treated. She was functioning well despite her horrifying childhood. She survived physical, sexual and emotional abuse perpetrated on her by her parents, primarily her father. She had some experience with EMDR and found it to be one of the treatments that had helped her over the years. She sought me out, and we began to work together.

She had not been to sleep before 2 a.m. in her entire life. You see, her father would tell his wife he was going to "check the house" to make sure everything was locked and secure. He never did this after 2 a.m., always before. He was a big man in his church, an anointed elder. She never told me what religion her family practiced, but she had nothing but disdain for religion and God. Who could blame her?

As a little girl, like many little girls who were being abused in the fifties and sixties, Barbara had one card to play. I am astonished at just how similar her story is to those of many other women and some men I have treated over the years. What is this card she could play? What is the move that would make this all stop? She would tell her mother. Mother would surely help her and make it all stop. Mother would protect her.

One day, while her father was at work, a day when she had just had enough and did not think she could endure any more of this abuse, she played her trump card. The eight-year-old finally told her mother. Her mother responded to the news by screaming, yelling and wailing: "Liar! Liar! Liar!"

Then her mother put her adult hands around the little girl's throat and choked her to death, or near death. The little girl passed out, went limp, and woke up in a dark closet, only to find her mother vacuuming on the other side of the closet door.

This is a common story. Often the adult in my office who shares this type of story summarizes her feelings about this betrayal by the mother in the same way: "My mother's unwillingness to help make this stop was far worse than the abuse itself." Barbara felt the same way.

Nothing was said, nothing changed, and the abuse continued for Barbara. Now in her late 40s, she was in my office, ready to do EMDR. She was a brave client. She went back into the gates of hell with these seemingly endless horrors. In one EMDR session, she began to itch all over her body. I had witnessed many bizarre things during EMDR sessions, but I had never witnessed such a thing before. The situation got worse before it got better. She began itching all over. Then she began to shake and scratch. She began talking in the process, which she'd never done before, asking me to help her. She asked, "What should I do?"

I said what I always say, "go with that," the body sensation. Really, I was thinking, "What the hell is going on with this?" This was one of those threshold moments.

You see, her father was particularly angry with Barbara one summer day for not finishing her lunch. She hated eggs, and he frequently forced her to eat them. She was about nine or ten at the time.

He ordered her to undress and get in the bathtub, and he proceeded to dump her beloved ant farm, one of her favorite possessions, all over her. She was attacked by the ants, hence the itching body sensation. We did not target this ant farm memory, and she did not remember it; it just emerged through her body during the EMDR processing. The itching stopped because her mother came to her and cleaned her off, rescued her, and put anti-itching salve on her.

This stopped the itching when she was a child, and the memory stopped the itching in my office. No one has ever been harmed by activating an EMDR memory. The person is alive and in my office, so whatever the memory was that they experienced, they survived it.

C.S. Lewis wrote in his book *Mere Christianity,* "The evil dictators in history are all so alike, but the Saints are all so unique and different."[11] The more I do this work, the more I agree. I would expand his thought, not limiting it to dictators but to any person who perpetuates evil. I treat women who have been or are in abusive relationships. It's like these men all went to the same university. They say the same things, do the same things; they are all so alike. Their victims are so resilient, brave, and unique.

The mothers who buried their head in the sand, Judas-like, are all the same. "What will happen if my husband goes to jail? How will I survive? I know. I'll act as if it's not happening." Hence they save their financial security but sacrifice the daughters.

After doing some EMDR, Barbara was sometimes able to fall asleep for the first time before 2 a.m. Some nights were still a struggle, and other nights, she did not give the time a second thought. In the end, many of her PTSD symptoms were subsiding. She was enjoying life more than she had in years. She was not riddled with fear. We ended our work together because she was doing so well.

About six months later, Barbara returned, angry at me because, although she no longer had any serious PTSD symptoms, she was unhappy, depressed, and confused about what to do with her life. Barbara felt betrayed, in a way.

"And furthermore, I had this stupid dream last night that really upset me," she said. "I was driving my brand-new car, and someone hit me from behind. I was not hurt, but the ambulance driver said I should go to the hospital to be examined just to make sure I was OK. So I went to the closest hospital, which was St. Elizabeth's Hospital. In the dream, I worked there. When I got there, I had apparently lost my identification. I did not remember my name, and the people at the hospital, whom I knew, said they did not know me, either.

"What the heck is that dream all about?" she continued. "I'll tell you one thing, I sure do feel lost, like I don't know who I am anymore. At least when I was afraid all the time, I knew who I was and why I was afraid."

I have a lot of experiences with dreams. I always ask my clients to write their dreams down as we go through this process. I thought to myself, what the hell is going on here? Barbara's PTSD symptoms were greatly reduced, almost completely gone, and she was still unhappy.

This was when the holiness of this work was presented to me, and after hearing that dream, I immediately understood. "You know, Barbara," I said, "that hospital could have been called anything. Your unconscious chose 'St. Elizabeth' as the name for the hospital for an important reason. Do you know who St. Elizabeth was?"

She responded with more irritation in her voice: "No. You know how I feel about God and religion. I have no interest in that stuff."

I thought, this is very strange or perhaps wonderful, because this changed the view of my work in a very profound way. It seemed we resolved old problems but had created new ones. These new ones became evident with a dream, a wondrous dream that immediately got my attention. She had no idea of the importance of this hospital name, but I did. In fact, once I figured out what was going on, I had my own personal "a-ha moment." St. Elizabeth is the mother of John the Baptist, the messenger of God who shall prepare the way for the Lord. He shall prepare the way for the one bringing the New Testament, the new way.

Additionally, the Blessed Virgin Mary visited St. Elizabeth while both were pregnant, St. Elizabeth with John the Baptist and the Virgin Mary with Jesus.

What does this have to do with anything? It has to do with everything. It changes everything. Through this religious symbolism, EMDR becomes an accelerated process that seems to sometimes open a portal to the divine.

This dream showed me clearly that there was more to my work than collecting symptoms, giving a diagnosis and providing a cookie-cutter treatment. This little dream along with the *Sometimes in Death a Friend You'll Find* dream began to profoundly change my view of my work, because I had done those three things very effectively (collect symptoms-diagnose-treat), but my client was back with a whole new and very different set of problems.

C.G. Jung said that "chaos and confusion are necessary ingredients for psychological transformation."[12] It is clear that Barbara was in a state of chaos and confusion, waiting for a sense of order and understanding to emerge. And it eventually did emerge in a beautiful and wonderful way.

The human connection is just as or even more valuable than the eye movements. One cannot just move one's eyes back and forth and be healed any more than a person can talk to themselves in the mirror empathetically; no, the human link is essential. This is one of those moments, a sharing of a dream the client experienced with the therapist, a dream that changed both of them. This event would dramatically support the notion that you must have a therapist to be healed by EMDR.

In graduate school, they teach you how to think. They have no use for dreams, wonder, mystery and God, not to mention other four-letter profanities like Jung, love, and soul. I have two master's degrees and a doctorate. I learned how to think. That's what they teach you, they teach you how to think and think some more. After all, I'm a psychologist, a practitioner of the science of the mind, and my mind has been saturated with the scientific method. They call people like me scientific-practitioners. My teachers taught me how to think and suffocated any exploration into the mystery and wonder of life.

I went to graduate school in my forties to continue a formal exploration into the mystery and wonder that I had experienced in my own life development.

My exploration began in the '70s, my *Red Book* years. For those of you who do not know what *The Red Book* is, you will by the end of this book. For now, it is the personal journal where C.G. Jung, the founder of Jungian psychology, encountered his soul or, if you will, his unconscious mind in very intimate and personal writings.

I, too, was invited to engage my inner life in an exploration in the '70s, and I have about thirty journals filled with

These are a few of my journals documenting my exploration inward.

these types of writings and explorations to prove it.

In 1976, my best friend was studying at Notre Dame University. He became very interested in Jungian psychology. I was studying music not far from there. I was in Chicago at Roosevelt University, right on Michigan Avenue — quite a culture shock for a young teen from a small steel town called Aliquippa, located on the Ohio River near Pittsburgh.

In 1978, John said I should start recording my dreams so we might discuss them together. He was friends with Morton T. Kelsey, a professor, Episcopalian minister and Jungian analyst at Notre Dame. He said Morton would help us out with this study of dreams.

John had been our high school valedictorian who never got a "B" in his life; I struggled. Music school was no different. It was a struggle. I remember saying: "John, I have enough trouble during the day without more bad news in my dreams at night. I do not need to know about how lost I am in this life of mine. I already know I'm lost and afraid."

Being the good friend that he was, he said, "OK, I understand."

The next night, I had the most terrifying nightmare I had ever had. Lee Harvey Oswald was jumping up and down on my bed and laughing at me. It continued night after night until I was afraid to go to sleep in my little Chicago apartment. Lee Harvey Oswald frightened me more than any other man. I was eight years old and in elementary school when he assassinated President Kennedy, and I did not sleep well for months after President Kennedy was killed. The Kennedy assassination would play an important symbolic role in my life some twenty years later. Lee Harvey Oswald invited me into this inner world of wonder, growth and horror.

I did not know what to do about this nightmare. I just knew I needed to sleep and to get rid of this terrifying nightly attack. So I did what I always did during those years when I needed advice. I called John, because he knew everything. Furthermore, at that time, he was the only guy I knew who had any idea about dreams.

I recounted the nightmare to him, and he asked Morton for advice.

"Morton said you should put a notebook by your bed and record your dreams," John told me. "You can start with the nightmare, and if you do, they'll probably stop." John continued to share Morton's thoughts, "You've been invited to this inner exploration for a reason you might not understand at this time. For now, you might as well accept it. Reject it, and you'll just have more nightmares."

This sounded like pure rubbish to me. I didn't do it the first night. I had the nightmare again. So I figured, what have I got to lose? I couldn't believe it, but he was right. I wrote the nightmare in a notebook and began examining my dreams. That nightmare never returned.

I worked with dreams from that day forward. Dreams have been an important part of my adult life. I know them so well, I rarely have to write them down anymore, because I know what they're saying. They're like old friends, symbols that have been an important part of my life for most of my life.

Perhaps I was invited all those years ago so I would be equipped to help clients, even though I had no idea I was going to become a psychologist some twenty-five years later. After all, I was studying music, not psychology.

These are mysterious events, and in my many years of attending to my inner life, wondrous things are a regular experience for me, in spite of the fact that graduate school almost destroyed my respect and love of the wondrous and sometimes miraculous workings of the human psyche — the human soul. I had forgotten about it for a while. I was a scientist, after all, no longer a man searching to understand his soul, the meaning of his life, and his God.

In graduate school, I experienced the danger that has come to fruition, a danger Jung warned against almost a hundred years ago: "Science is not, indeed, a perfect instrument, but it is a superior and indispensable one that works harm *only when taken as an end in itself*."[13] [Italics mine]

The St. Elizabeth Hospital dream brought me back to my roots of psychological inquiry, back when I was that young man studying music. I could no longer ignore what I had always known and experienced in my life, that the wondrous workings of the soul are real and powerful. It is the most privileged work and the most gratifying. I had experienced many wondrous and powerful experiences in my more than three decades of dream work and active imagination explorations. This inward journey has helped me greatly in my work, in my life, and in my relationship with God, therefore helping me in my relationship with others.

This St. Elizabeth's dream hit me like a sledgehammer. An inner voice said to me as I pondered this wondrous dream: "You know this is the truth. You cannot work like a machine any longer. You've been preparing your entire life for sharing what you learned over the last thirty years, and cookie-cutter psychology ain't it."

It is amazing to me that this dream, which was not even my dream, began to change my client's life as well as my view of my work. It also began to change my view of the psychological process that EMDR greatly accelerated. This dream changed all of these things in relatively short order. I was returning to the view I had lived by for thirty years but had forgotten. I had traded in the mystery, majesty and wonder of the human psyche for a secular scientific career.

I began re-reading all those books I consumed with vigor in my twenties and thirties. I examined all the sections I had underlined as well as the multitude of notes I had crammed into the margins. This return to these profoundly beautiful books was an eye-opener. I was shocked to realize just how much of my thinking was in those books. I apparently had not been thinking as my graduate school training had led me but, rather, I had returned to the way of mystery and wonder.

I saw underlined sections that I often repeated verbatim to my clients. It was clear that I had not completely abandoned the wonder and mystery of my work; it was leaking out in therapy sessions whenever the client would benefit from these ideas.

Surprisingly, this change was all out of my awareness. Living as a Jungian Christian for most of my life seems to have embedded many of these ideas in my soul, and no amount of graduate school was going to destroy who I was and how I thought. Now, it was time to embrace it fully. Although not without reservation. Psychology rejects religion for the most part and religion rejects psychology. This book is an attempt to unify both, which may cause a rejection from both. I hope, however, that it will unify and the synergistic healing power of these two disciplines united will be embraced and realized.

I do not want to give the impression that graduate school is a bad thing. Truth be told, I loved my experience there. I enjoyed my relationships with fellow students and professors. It was stimulating in a number of ways. I became aware of things of which I had little or no knowledge, after which I was free to reject or accept what was taught there.

Graduate school is what it is supposed to be, a place where science is revered, and this scientific work is important. It is essential. It is, however, important to know that it is not the only thing nor is it the only way. It is a necessary piece but not sufficient to be an end in itself. Much as Jung stated about the dangers with science, it is the same with graduate school: It is dangerous only if one thinks there is nothing else.

The St. Elizabeth dream created an awakening in me. It catapulted me back to where I began, except knowing that inner world at a much deeper level, perhaps because of the thirty years of life experience behind me, perhaps because of all I was taught in graduate school.

Perhaps it was being a father and a husband. Perhaps it was a deeper and richer experience of my religious faith. Perhaps it was all of this that created a much more mature and less naïve view of the world, of God, of my work, and of people.

When I was explaining this experience to my old friend John, the same John who was instrumental in introducing me to this journey over thirty years ago, he said it's like "Little Gidding." Like I said, John knows just about everything. I queried, "What the hell is a little gidding?"

"It's a poem by T. S. Eliot," he said.

I am a lover of poetry but had never heard of this one. I was familiar with *The Wasteland* and most everyone has heard of *Old Possum's Book of Practical Cats,* on which the musical "Cats" is based, but "Little Gidding" — never heard of it. He emailed me four lines from that rather lengthy poem. He thought they would resonate with me and my present experience, and he was right; those lines made the hairs on the back of my neck stand up. It basically says you'll end up in life where you began, but toward the end of your life you will see it clearly for the first time.

Sometimes poets say things in a few lines that an entire book cannot explain. If you do not understand the significance of these lines, then you are too young, but trust me, you will understand at some time in your life. Perhaps the world of psychology also needs to return to where it began and come to know it for the first time.

Barbara was not in my office because her symptoms had returned, but rather because she did not know who she was without her anxiety and fear.

I worked with her and discovered that there are six stages to this EMDR transformational process. Barbara was in my office again because she was in a state of confusion and chaos, which I call Stage Four. Jung knew all about this, but these days, therapy rarely goes beyond stage three because it does not completely dismantle the negative belief, it only treats it and helps the patient cope with it. We had completed the first three stages in our initial work. I realized in working with her that it is the follow-up work in this second phase, which includes the discovery of the new identity, that is perhaps the most important work of all.

Working with Barbara gave me a comprehensive view of the entire process of transformation for the first time. The St. Elizabeth dream clearly indicated to me that my clients were experiencing a stage that was new to me — a loss of identity. This included her internal reality, working with dreams and symbols that follow a consistent pattern from stage to stage. We also had to address struggles out in the world and with her behavior, adapting to the new positive core belief. Finally, EMDR continued to reduce emotional distress and psychological and spiritual blocks that would come up from time to time.

Here is a review of the six stages originally shared in our map of the soul:

Stage One:	Avoidance
Stage Two:	Surrender
Stage Three:	Removal of symptoms/destroying the old self
Stage Four:	Loss of identity/chaos and confusion
Stage Five:	Rebirth
Stage Six:	Renewal, acceptance, and assimilation of the new way

What is the significance? St. Elizabeth held in her womb John the Baptist, the one who "prepares the way of the Lord." In a way, Barbara was in labor, experiencing a psychological pregnancy as she waited for the rebirth of her new self. She had to spend some time in a state of confusion, waiting for the rebirth. Waiting for the new way to emerge.

During pregnancy, there is a sense of waiting and anticipating something wonderful that is coming into the world. Life is suspended, but a lot is going on underneath the surface. It is a time of patience, a time where one can only wait and prepare for the birth. So it is with the rebirth of the new psychological self. There is a period of suspended animation when preparations have to be done quietly and internally.

Now, after reflecting for some time on this dream and working with clients who were experiencing this confused state, I began to notice the parallel in these six stages to six moments in Christ's passion. Let's take a look at this startling comparison, which is a map — perhaps a map of the psyche, perhaps a map of the soul — but it is a map that many of my patients follow with consistency.

Having a map does a couple of things. First, it lets the client know I have a clear understanding of this process and that I have accompanied others on this journey. It also provides a sense of relief that others have felt the way they feel and have experienced what they are experiencing.

These six stages can be viewed in psychological terms or in Christian terms. There are also similarities in Islam and Kabbalah. For now, let's look at the Christian parallel. The Christian perspective is important, because if the client believes in God and is a Christian, it gives significant meaning to one's suffering. Then this distress clients are experiencing is not meaningless, but rather a "cross" they must carry to their crucifixion in order to become reborn.

It also helps them understand that the distress they are feeling is not permanent but temporary and that this distress has value. One client said to me: "I guess, doc, as Christians, we are no different than Christ. We, too, must suffer in our lives to grow into a better, wiser and perhaps holier Christian."

This transformational experience, initiated by confusion and emotional distress, must be understood and not dismissed or medicated away. Through a spiritual lens, it becomes a creative and sacred process.

The Christian six-stage parallel is presented below:

Stage One: Gethsemane.   (Avoidance)
"Father, if it be possible,
let this cup pass from me."

Stage Two: Surrender to God's will.   (Surrender)
"Not my will, but yours."

Stage Three: Crucifixion.   (EMDR)
Destroying the old self.

Stage Four: Three days in the tomb.   (Chaos/Loss of identity; period of creative introversion)

Stage Five: Resurrection.   (Rebirth)

Stage Six: Ascension.   (Renewal)
Christ accepts his
transfigured body.

It is important to remember that we are describing psychological and spiritual experiences. Therefore, the road is not usually linear or logical. A person can be in more than one stage at the same time.

Additionally, one can retreat and move backward to a stage previously navigated. There often is a temporary retreat to the old way. This happens almost without exception.

Although it is important to arrive at the final stage to complete the process, the way one gets there varies from person to person.

You may have guessed by now that Nicole, who had to get permission from her pastor in order for me to treat her, was armed with the Christian six-stage model. Her pastor was surprised by this model.

He had no idea that there was a psychologist in town who was willing to value the Christian journey in his work with clients who desire to include this in their work with me. I don't know if it was my work or Nicole's experience that convinced him. Initially, she had a good understanding of what EMDR was supposed to do, and she had a willingness to explain it all to him because she really wanted to try EMDR. Whatever it was that convinced him, she got what she needed, and I was able to help her be rid of the panic attacks by doing what I do.

6

A Closer Look at the Six Stages

In his book *Inner Gold*, Jungian psychotherapist, sometimes monk, and lover of Indian spirituality Robert A. Johnson tells us that his first analyst and Jungian trainer, Fritz Kunkel, told him there are three ways to study psychology: "Read Greek Mythology, read Jung, or watch. Watching is best."[14]

In my work over this past decade, "watching" has been my primary method, with reading Jung a close second, following Kunkel's suggestion. This has brought forth some interesting fruit.

I noticed that consistent patterns in this transformational work are predictable, as the client proceeds through the stages. These patterns exist in all aspects of their lives.

In my "watching," I discovered the stages. Perhaps I had a sense of this process because I had gone through something like them in my late thirties, when I had had a terrible, difficult struggle leading to my personal transformation and rebirth, a treacherous journey I do not care to repeat.

In a way, I had been preparing to see this six-stage pattern all my life, and there it was. After three decades of study and introspection, it was right in front of my eyes. Saint Elizabeth, John the Baptist, and the Mother and the Son of God found their way into my office by way of a confused client, who had no interest in God, religion, or her dream: an unlikely combination in a therapist's office in Florida to encounter the divine.

There is power in religious language, and the belief that these difficult periods are indeed sacred and holy is no small thing.

When I am working with someone who believes in God, for example a Christian like Nicole, I can say to her: "You must carry your cross to your personal crucifixion in order to be reborn and healed. It is a misnomer that being 'Born Again' is a warm and fuzzy experience."

This is a far more meaningful and profound statement to a Christian than: "We will use this cognitive behavioral treatment and that should reduce your symptoms. Perhaps you should call your doctor for some medication." I do recommend medication sometimes, and I use cognitive strategies as well. These are necessary resources to manage symptoms until EMDR can cure them.

To repeat, it is important to remember that in describing psychological and spiritual experiences, the road is not always nice and neat. A person can be in more than one stage at the same time. Additionally, one can move backward to a stage that was seemingly completed. Clients often feel a need to return to the old way.

EMDR creates insight for such clients. They can no longer go back to the world of what they knew, because it does not look the same. They are no longer ignorant of their reality, so they can no longer live in a world where *ignorance is bliss.* After the transformational work of EMDR, ignorance no longer exists.

It is very common to be in multiple stages simultaneously, especially stages three, four, and five. Working with the soul means dealing with eternal language and multilevel experiences. The soul is not limited to time and space, and neither is this process.

For example, the St. Elizabeth dream is a prime example of a symbol that may work on multiple levels in a number of different ways that may affect many people. Even you, reading these words, may be affected in a transformational way by this little dream.

The symbol of St. Elizabeth in Barbara's dream affected me profoundly in spiritual, religious, and psychological ways, both personally and vocationally, as it changed the way I saw all subsequent clients, and it brought me back to where I had come from when I had jotted down my first dreams in 1978. It reminded me of the profound power of our dreams and the unconscious.

Symbols are eternal and far richer with meaning and power than intellectual thinking and abstract theories, which are necessary but not sufficient.

With these truths in mind, let's look in more detail at the six stages.

Stage One: Avoidance (Gethsemane)

Sometimes the most challenging part of my job is describing the EMDR process and convincing clients that EMDR actually works. Even as they sit in front of me, the person who is going to help them change, the person whom they've waited two or three months to see, they remain in the land of avoidance. They resist change.

Frequently these clients are sent by a friend who gave them a glowing endorsement of my work and of EMDR, yet they remain in Gethsemane, afraid to proceed. They tell me that those things that happened to them as a child do not bother them now. They inform me that those old events have nothing to do with their present problems. In the end, they usually decide to give EMDR a try, mainly because they are in such emotional distress that they are willing to try anything to get relief.

Resistance is part of the process. New clients are at the very beginning of the journey. They do not know it yet, but once they set foot in my office, they are in the land of transformation. Once their soul, or psyche, gets a sense of this reality, that the old way is about to be dismantled, it will not be denied. There is no turning back.

Clients will often have an experience like mine when I was invited by John to honor my dreams, but I resisted, and so I was attacked by my soul. Nightmare after nightmare occurred, until I began to tread the path that was offered to me.

This human characteristic of avoidance was modeled

for us by Christ as he, too, tried to avoid his reality: "My Father, if it be possible, let this cup pass from me.."[15]

He tried to deny his reality. We know that, at least for a moment, he wanted to act as if he could just walk away and forget he was the son of God, who was born to die a horrible death. Who could blame him?

This sentence was spoken for us, not because he really wanted to walk away, and not because he thought he could. This was perhaps the most human moment Christ experienced in the New Testament; this is perhaps the most human statement he ever uttered. He wanted to avoid his authentic path. Wanting to avoid and deny one's reality is what most of us do for much of our lives. Christ expressed this human side of his reality to show us it's OK to avoid pain for a while, but not for our entire lives.

Some of my clients are in their seventies, and they think, why is this happening to me at my age? This work has to be done. It is an eternal task, and the soul cares nothing about your chronological age.

I am not the first psychologist to see a Christian parallel as an important model for reconciling human psychological struggles. Morton Kelsey, the Jungian analyst and Episcopalian minister my friend knew, discusses this avoidance stage in his book *Encounter with God,* quoting Jung as well:

"The growing awareness of the inferior part of the personality (the old ineffective self)," Jung wrote, " . . . should not be twisted into an intellectual activity, for it has far more meaning of a suffering and a passion that implicates the whole person."

Kelsey continues: "Dealing with the unconscious contents can be a painful process which most people will avoid if they can. This emphasis on creative suffering has much in common with the teachings of Jesus of Nazareth."[16]

I often say that EMDR is like Jungian depth psychology on steroids. EMDR moves into unconscious connections with laser-like speed and accuracy. EMDR accesses hidden material that the Jungian analysts would call "the shadow" (that which is hidden from our awareness), which EMDR brings to awareness, and dismantles these connections quickly and efficiently. It very quickly reconciles the negative effects of these maladaptive beliefs. Once the EMDR process is set in motion, the transformation process begins. Death starts and gradually moves to rebirth. The sequence of Christ's Passion is under way, and there is no turning back.

Stage Two: Surrender
(surrender to God's will)

Surrender is the moment when the client agrees to proceed. This can come after minutes, a few weeks, or years. Usually when a client shows up in my office, they have been invited. Their souls have created such intense levels of distress in their lives that they have no choice but to seek relief. It is a distressing sort of invitation, but an invitation nonetheless.

They are ready to surrender to the journey. When EMDR is used, they must surrender. They must allow themselves to take the journey in order to change and allow the transformation to emerge.

Each person has a different feeling about change. Clients all come into my office wanting to change, sometimes just to get rid of their panic attacks or their depressive symptoms. Sometimes they have a sense that the way they have been dealing with their lives is not working. They aren't sure why, but they know that things are not going well.

At this stage, I give an explanation of the six stages of the journey. Sometimes I give it in secular, scientific language, and sometimes in religious language. It depends on the client's belief system, not mine. Usually, people are willing to start the journey after a map of the work is laid out carefully and sincerely for them. If they have confidence and trust in their therapist, they will proceed. Of course, the distressing emotional states they are in are also a great help in motivating them to change. "I'll do anything! Just help me feel better, doc."

The Christian view is relevant here, as Christ followed his wish to avoid his destiny, only to accept it in the next breath. He went from avoidance to acceptance and surrender immediately:

Avoidance: "My Father, if it be possible, let this cup pass from me."

Surrender: "Unless I drink it, may your will be done." (Matt: 26:42)

Humans take a bit more time than Christ did to move from avoidance to surrender. It can take decades. Some of us never even get to stage two. Some spend their entire lives in ignorance and avoidance, looking outward for the cause of their problems, rather than having the courage to look inward to find change and transformation, unable to bravely question themselves, saying, "Maybe it's me?"

Human organisms are hard-wired to avoid pain. We are very skilled at avoiding discomfort. Conventional wisdom says that emotion is something strong people should just "get over," and move on.

Nothing is farther from the truth. Emotions drive our every decision in life, and the less we are aware of this fact, the more we are a ship in a storm without a rudder or compass. Our denial and ignorance wreak havoc in every aspect of our lives. We think we are making good decisions, but instead we are simply creating scenarios that replicate our past history and perpetuate dissatisfaction. Our template is set in childhood in an often adaptive way, but later in life this template becomes ineffective. Unfortunately we do not notice it; therefore, we have no idea we need to change it until trouble begins.

EMDR requires more than a letting go. Clients must allow the soul to move without intention. The ultimate surrender is required. Jung writes in *The Red Book,* "Do you still not know that the way to truth stands open only to those without intentions?"[17]

Clients must trust me, because I am asking a lot of them. They must take a path through their often horrifying pasts, allowing EMDR to activate their thoughts, feelings, images, memories, and even body sensations of these terrible experiences. EMDR reactivates the past trauma, if only briefly.

Complete surrender to the process is required, with no intent. This is the only way the journey will take them where they need to go. This is no easy feat for clients who do not easily trust anyone or anything. Earning their trust can be a challenge, but I present them with a map of the six stages, and that goes a long way in the service of gaining their trust. They are surprised to know that I have accompanied hundreds on this path. Some weep when they understand that this is a holy journey, one we all should take. A session here is not chitchat; it is deadly serious stuff.

Stage Three: Dismantling of the old self (crucifixion)

One of the most difficult parts of the journey is dismantling the old self. The now maladaptive personality is no longer working for the client; therefore, it must be destroyed. This is a psychological crucifixion, and it feels like one, as you can see by the horribly difficult work Georgia did in the first chapter.

Taking this journey is stressful for the therapist as well as the client. Even though I have accompanied hundreds of people on this journey, often there are twists and turns that I have never seen before. Many things happen that are unexpected. It all is a mystery. Just when you think you have seen it all, something else happens. So stage three is "the work."

Jungian analyst Sanford describes the anxiety-provoking process:

> This process of psychological dissolution is, in
> practice, often a frightening time, for when we feel
> our old personality dissolving we are not always
> confident that something else is coming to take its
> place. At this point a certain amount of faith is re-
> quired as well as, quite often, the moral and psy-
> chological assistance of another person.[18]

Stage three work is ridding the person of the original symptoms. There is a great deal of time spent in dealing with wounds from the past. It also dismantles the lifelong negative core belief, which is a good thing, but it can be a frightening process, as Sanford describes.

It is not unusual for clients to feel overwhelmed in this stage. This is the stage in which insight occurs. They see things for what they are and realize they have been on the wrong path for a very long time. Some say, "I feel like I've been asleep for 50 years." I reassure them that everything they have been through was necessary.

Stage Four: Loss of Identity (three days in the tomb)

As you remember, Barbara completed stage three and was feeling good. She could not believe how much all her fears and anxieties had been reduced or eliminated. Then, however, she returned with her St. Elizabeth's dream.

Unfortunately, Barbara was not unique. The peace after completing stage three work often does not last, because these symptoms have been companions for decades, and once they are eliminated, the person often feels lost and confused. Jung said, "Chaos and confusion are essential ingredients for psychological transformation." This period of internal chaos is stage four. He was correct, and with EMDR, this period begins soon after stage three seems to be resolved.

Stage Four surprises clients; even when I warn them about it, they often do not believe me. They say things like, "If I'm no longer depressed or anxious or fearful, I'll be happy, doc."

Then they are hit with a strong dose of chaos and confusion, a loss of identity, and a terrifying sense of facing the unknown. It is Christ's three days in the tomb and his descent into hell. They can do nothing here except a great deal of inner work: EMDR processing and talking about the new person. Clients often say they feel as if they are in limbo. Who will this person be? What will this person do? John Sanford says a period of creative introversion is needed.

When this stage first started to appear in my clients, I was surprised. As far as I knew, once stage three was complete, I was finished. EMDR had removed all pathology. Everything clients wanted when they initially came in to see me had been accomplished. No more anxiety, no more flashbacks. So what's the problem?

Well, one of my trainers tells the story of a veteran he

treated successfully. He was surprised that the veteran did not seem happy about the work. The veteran said to him, "Doc, if I am no longer a disabled veteran, then who the hell am I?"

I had forgotten this story until I started to hear it from my clients. Wow! I was shocked when I first started to hear this kind of complaint from my clients. Now what was I supposed to do? Should I help them heal completely? Or should I partially heal them, and then stop, so they could keep some troubles in their psyche? I had always looked at this work as a death-rebirth sequence. This was a twist that I had not anticipated.

The truth became obvious. In stage four, the client experiences a period of chaos and confusion. A very real loss of identity occurs, and words cannot describe the anguish that clients sometimes feel.

They have to let go of the known self, the part of them that is creating problems for them in their life, often horrible problems, but in a way this is the devil they know, which feels safer than the unknown.

It is very, very tough to discover that what you've been doing for the last thirty years is all wrong. Resistance is a natural response to this reality. However, when clients say that they have wasted most of their lives, I reject this idea completely. Nothing is wasted; it is all a necessary part of the journey.

Stage Five: Rebirth (resurrection)

This is a period when the clients get a glimpse of the new way. It is rebirth experienced intermittently. They begin to engage the world differently, they begin to see themselves differently, and they begin to view others differently. Nevertheless, even though they get a taste of this new and more adaptive way to be, they usually retreat to the old way briefly. They fight to hang on to the old way, but they also fight to let go of the old way, as they reach bravely for the new way. It is a Herculean struggle.

Fortunately, they can never go back to the old way, because they could only tolerate it because they were unaware of what was going on. They were completely controlled by unconscious behaviors. Once insight occurs, they can never go back, although they try. Once they have had a taste of health and normalcy, they cannot retreat to the old way permanently.

Stage Six: Assimilation and acceptance of the new self (ascension)

Stage Six is the end of a long, hard journey. Here the client has become accustomed to the new way. A sense of calm and peace sets in. Clients are completely accepting of themselves. They are their authentic selves. They know who they are, where they are going, and who they want to come along with them.

They have changed their view of the world, their view

of themselves, and their view of others. They can now also change the way they engage the world, and the way in which they allow the world to engage them.

They no longer overreact to criticism and no longer fear disappointing others. They know in every cell of their beings that they are doing the best that they can do, and that that is good enough. It is a profoundly powerful place to be.

7

Tales from Stage One: Avoidance

Many clients want to stay in Stage One. They do not want to drink from the cup. Conventional wisdom says that strong people should just get over distressing emotions, so clients try to push these emotional wounds aside. "Just try not to think about it; stop worrying," they tell themselves. "There are so many people who are much worse off than I am."

Few people have any interest in allowing themselves to visit past horrifying events, the most painful moments of their lives. They say things like: "Doc, I spent my whole life trying to forget this stuff, and now you're saying you want me to re-experience it? I don't want to do that. Can't we just talk about my boss, who is driving me crazy?" Or: "That was a long time ago; I never think of that. That's not why I'm having panic attacks."

These clients are in my office because part of them knows something needs to change. Even though they are in front of me, taking time out of their day to go through this process, as well as paying me for my time, they still will often initially resist. Remember, even Christ modeled stage one for us.

Over the years, I have always been surprised at how often I am fooled by clients who seem to be doing serious work, but in reality, they are withholding the most important thing. They have been telling themselves their whole lives, "Oh, that was no big deal; I'm over that." So they exclude it from our work and from me.

These experiences they keep secret are often horrific traumas, such as rape, abortion, kidnapping, and sexual and physical abuse. I have treated clients who barely survived murder attempts on their lives, car accidents in which they almost died, or accidents where a person close to them did die. These memories are often buried, but they are not forgotten. They affect these brave clients every day, but the clients experience only the emotion. They do not get the context in a clear way. Often feelings are triggered by something that is symbolically similar, as we saw with Nicole, so the connection is never made.

In any case, the clients are here. They are in front of me. They took time out of their lives to see me. Usually because they have waited for a long time, sometimes years, even decades, now they are in extreme distress and have no idea why. They do not come to see someone like me unless nothing else has helped. I am the "what have I got to lose" guy.

This avoidance stage may have started decades ago. It often starts immediately after the event, and sometimes even in the midst of the event. People use mental gymnastics to keep this reality at bay, mechanisms like minimizing the importance of an event or repressing the memory completely. They can act as if the event never took place, or as if the event has had no lasting effect. Sometimes they re-write the history of the event in their mind, changing it so it's not so bad.

It is of no use to tell them how their past is affecting them in the present. They must experience the insight on their own. Attempts to explain the way this all works are not accepted. Lectures by the therapist are a waste of time.

Sooner or later, however, the defenses that keep these memories at bay begin to weaken, and the result is often some sort of emotional problem that seems to come out of nowhere, for no reason, like depression, panic attacks, anxiety, or irrational fears, like being afraid to drive in traffic or get on an airplane — something the client has always been able to do. Now these relatively routine behaviors are impossible to perform. Clients do not understand, and they are often desperate.

There comes a time when clients have had enough. The memories reach up, grab them and disable them. The coping mechanisms no longer work. This is their day, the day when they have been invited to an encounter with their soul, an encounter with Christ. They have been invited to their crucifixion and rebirth. They must change and move into their authentic selves, because anything is better than where they are at the moment. They have been invited.

John Sanford says: "Precisely those who seem least fit for the kingdom are those who come to enter into it. Those who are forced by life to concede to themselves that they are psychologically crippled, maimed, or blind can be compelled to enter in the great feast."[19]

Many expect to be healed without the dark journey backward. It is unfair that they must take this bloody road back to be healed. These courageous people who drink from this cup have often suffered years and years of torment. They should get a pass and be healed. They have suffered enough. Regrettably, though, that's not the way it works.

More traditional methods of therapy help them cope during this process. Cognitive strategies, behavioral approaches and relaxation can all be beneficial.

The most difficult work is here, at stage one. Once they allow themselves to begin, there is almost some immediate benefit. They know they are changing; they know this is something very real and profound. They know they are moving toward their truth, but it is very hard and painful work.

Morton Kelsey tells us: "People who claim to have had an experience of Christ which only made them feel wonderful, full of goose bumps and happy, may be imagining a Christ of their own making. Christ forces us to deal honestly with ourselves and thus makes it possible for us to deal honestly with others."[20]

Thomas A. Kempis supports this idea as well. He says in his book *The Imitation of Christ,* "There are many who are willing to share in Christ's kingdom, but few are willing to bear his cross."[21]

EMDR takes people to their truths, no matter how dark and treacherous those truths are, and brings them out of this darkness into a peaceful place, a place of wholeness.

Fortunately, it does this distressing work at the speed of thought.

Sanford tells us in his book *Healing and Wholeness*, "Anything rejected in the unconscious turns against us; on the other hand, to give conscious energy to the contents of the unconscious is to begin to win their positive energy and support."[22]

One of my clients was a powerful businesswoman. Her unconscious was an adversary, because she denied her emotional reality. She was a successful saleswoman, traveling all over the country for her company, teaching others to be as successful as she was.

One day her father died. Her mother said only five words to her before she walked into the funeral home. "Be strong and don't cry." She obeyed her mother and denied her emotional reality.

That night, she had her first panic attack. She became plagued with anxiety. She could not fly in an airplane or drive in traffic without panic attacks.

She came to see me. We targeted her father's death. She cried and grieved over her father's death, and the panic left her. The ignorance our society has in regard to the power of emotion is staggering. "Just pretend you don't feel; that's all you have to do" equates to total lack of understanding and respect for the devastating power of emotion.

Some of my clients mark their work with rituals, often before they walk into my office, without realizing what they are doing or why. A ritual sends the message to the unconscious, or your soul, that you are willing to do this emotional work. In this way, the soul becomes an ally, assisting by providing symbols and dreams. If you choose to deny the issues that must be examined and reconciled, the unconscious will attack using the mysterious power of emotion to cause internal distress until we work to understand what needs to change in our lives. This often is the source of pathology like depression, panic, and anxiety.

Getting a haircut is often a powerful ritual component in the process of change. The popular makeover, including cutting the overgrown hair of men and women, creating an entirely new look, often brings these people to tears. They are experiencing the symbolic power of change.

Tattoos are not uncommon expressions of the soul. A number of patients used them to mark the beginning of a troubled journey. Brothers in war will sometimes get tattoos together. You will read about my clients Tony and Ron who made the decision to engage this ritual. They both had these tattoos done before they entered my office.

One of my first clients was a brilliant young woman, a writer and teacher at a university. She documented our work together in her writings and in her journal. Her reflections on our work were beautiful, and she has given me permission to share her thoughts on both rituals, her haircut and her tattoo. Both of these acts occurred before our first meeting. She had no idea that her unconscious was preparing her for an encounter with her unconscious. It was assisting her long before she decided to call for an appointment.

Most of our work surrounded her father, a Vietnam veteran who was aloof and uninterested in her life. He had wanted a boy but was stuck with this girl. Tragically, I do not think he ever got to know his brilliant, courageous, and remarkable daughter.

There's a saying among therapists. We ask the question, "What is the opposite of love?" Everyone responds "hate," thinking, *That's a stupid question.* It's a trick question, because the answer is not "hate." The answer is "indifference."

Research bears this out. If children are ignored as if they do not exist, they often fare far worse than their abused counterparts. Both of these parenting styles are horrible, and both get terrible results, but it does seem that those who are ignored do worse.

My writer client was a miracle, because she overcame a life of indifference. She had no idea that the rituals she recently had performed were related to our work, because she had done the rituals before we met. Her unconscious took her by the hand and prepared her for this work. She was in stage three the minute she stepped into my office. She had surrendered long before I met her.

If one opens the lines of communication between the conscious and the unconscious, powerful and transformative moments can occur, even when the process is working outside one's awareness.

My client would not have been open to following her intuition had she not been experienced with her inner self. She is a writer who avidly kept a journal. Journaling about her life, her loves, her emotional reality — these inner reflections were as much a part of her life as eating and sleeping.

When that which is hidden becomes revealed, a powerful upheaval of energy moves the transformative process forward. Psychotherapists are privileged to witness these creative moments as we provide a creative space for our clients, allowing them to create and experience these moments.

My bright and creative client was, and I am sure, still is, a gifted writer who spent much of her life trying to get her father's attention, without success. She came to therapy in an attempt to come to terms with the state of this relationship.

She wrote about beginning the process of therapy. She had unknowingly begun the process of making our therapeutic encounter sacred and holy by using two rituals with symbolic power to help her understand what she was about to undertake. She wrote the following passage after she understood the meaning of her behaviors:

> Freshly enlisted soldiers have all their hair cut off as a rite of passage into the role of protector. Buddhist monks often shave their heads before entering a monastery to erase any vanity. The day I cut my hair I stood balanced on a precipice between these two roles of warrior and spiritual pupil. "You sure you wanna do this?" the stylist asked me as I returned to her after the shampoo. I ran my hands through my wet hair, starting at the scalp and moving downward through the ten or twelve inches of

my beautiful keystone. It was now golden brown from summer sun, fragrant with the salon's apple shampoo.

I looked at myself in the mirror, my hair framing my face, and thought about how it moved with me when I danced and how ex-boyfriends used to bury their noses in it before falling asleep, but there was a difference between who I was and who I needed to be. My eyes wandered to the magazine clipping I brought in, a picture of a Winona Ryder look-alike with short, cropped hair.

"Yes, please, I want it like the picture." I sat down and closed my eyes and tried not to wince as I heard the metallic scrape of the scissors opening and closing. After a few minutes, I opened my eyes. The other patrons were looking on with expressions of shock and curiosity as clumps of my silken tresses fell to the floor. The scissors moved mercilessly around my head. I thought of Henry Miller saying that freedom comes from cutting yourself free from the past and suddenly I was afraid I was cutting too much and if that woman cut one more strand of hair I would lift out of the chair and float away. I squeezed my eyes shut against my mirror image.

When it was over I thanked the stylist with downcast eyes and slipped out of the chair. I paid and watched her sweep mounds of my hair into a

dustbin and then carry it back to the salon out of
my sight. I bit my lip, said a quick prayer and left
the salon, trying to make myself invisible.

This young woman had created a powerful ritual for
beginning the process of therapy. As a writer, she had regularly journaled and enjoyed solitude, so that piece of the
process was already in place. She also informed me that
around the time she had had her hair cut she had had a tattoo done of a Korean Dragon, which she explained protect-
ed warriors during battle. She told me about these acts after
a few therapy sessions, and we explored and understood
them. The excerpt you just read was written months after
the actual haircut had been done.

When she told me about these two ritual events, I asked
her: "What is the first thing that happens when a newly en-
listed soldier arrives for training at boot camp? What do you
think the first thing that happened to your dad was when he
arrived that first day at boot camp in the 1960s?"

She looked at me with tears in her eyes and said: "They
get their hair cut. The soldiers all get their hair cut before
they go to war."

For her, therapy was the battleground and her father
her opponent. One year later, after her hair had grown back
somewhat and her treatment with me had been completed,
she emerged victorious. This young female warrior was not
going to have it any other way.

She had begun with an ordinary haircut. The only reminder she had of this event was a lock of her cut hair,

which she taped to her journal — a symbol that there was no longer a need for a sword.

It was now OK to lay down her arms and accept her father for who he was, because, no matter what he thinks of her, he does not define her in any way. She is beautiful, bright, and she is a writer. She feels "good enough."

The poet Robert Bly warns of the loss of ritual in our society. He says in his book *Iron John*:

> The Catholic church remembered ritual space in the Latin Mass, but for Protestants it fell into oblivion. With exceptions, Protestantism has spread its ignorance of ritual space everywhere in the world. Living in an age that has lost the concept [of ritual], we can easily make two mistakes: we provide no ritual space at all in our lives, and remain "cool"; or we stay in it too long. Some fundamentalists insist on remaining for forty years in ritual space without an exit — no sloppy humanness allowed.[23]

Rituals are powerful and a way to stay in touch with our individual and collective soul. I wanted to touch on this subject because our society is void of them. This is a tragic loss, and it must be reclaimed, because it is essential in Stage Four: the loss and search for one's identity. Finding one's new self is a solitary, introverted task, and ritual can assist in this interior work.

Journaling, working with dreams, and spending time

alone in solitude exploring the majesty of the inner world is essential for this time in stage four. Many resist, and usually there is trouble for those who resist, as you will see a little later in this book. I will also give some tips on what to do while in stage four: how to use a journal, work with dreams, and use active imagination techniques.

8

Another Face of Avoidance

Caroline came into my office with an irrational fear to which she was clearly overreacting. She was thirty-four years old, tall, attractive and well-groomed, wearing casual yet stylish attire. She wore appropriate make-up, and her hair was blond and always styled fashionably. She had tanned skin, and she had a great smile.

There was anxiety and urgency in her voice when we first met. I had successfully treated her six months earlier for anxiety, but she had returned with the same fears as before, only worse.

She said: "I have become terrified of thunderstorms. As you know, I've lived in Florida most of my life. I have been through hurricanes, tornadoes, and I have seen thousands of thunderstorms in my Florida life. I never gave them a second thought; I just dealt with them. Now I have to watch The Weather Channel all day long; I'm afraid to leave the house if there is a slight chance of rain, which in Florida is an everyday occurrence.

"You helped me six months ago. Now I do not know why these symptoms have returned, and they are worse than before. I did not think they could get worse, but they are worse. I think about thunderstorms all day and all night."

She continued with a sense of desperation in her voice: "Dr. Dobo, I'm going crazy. If there is a storm, I panic and call my husband and insist that he come home to be with me, which is crazy. I know he can't leave work. He's a fireman. He can't just come home every time it rains. What is wrong with me? Why is this happening again to me?"

It is rare for a patient to return for the same set of symptoms after comprehensive EMDR work. Caroline had completed a very detailed timeline, and we did a lot of work together to bring her to a place of contentment.

I was thinking, however, that she'd never really left Gethsemane. There was something she was not telling me, something she was unaware of or was unwilling to divulge in therapy. Clearly, her unconscious was still very much an adversary.

Resistance by clients to share a shameful event is common. I always remind them that they do not have to share what the event is, they just have to have an image of it in their mind's eye to begin this work. An image and a negative cognition, and we can get to work. I do not need to know what it is about. Nevertheless, sometimes not only is the memory too difficult to share, but it is too difficult for the client even to admit it ever happened.

As I have said, the soul wants us to look at that which is hidden — the Jungian shadow. Once this process begins, it is almost impossible to stop until all of the work is complete and that which needs to be revealed is revealed and addressed.

John A. Sanford, Jungian analyst and Episcopal minister, wrote over forty years ago in his book *The Kingdom Within*: "At some point in our inner development, there may be a desire on our part to stop the creative process, to decide 'This is enough; I need go no further.' Often there then sets in a time of darkness and confusion worse than the first. Such an experience is a sure sign that the creative process of the kingdom of God *will not* be denied."[24]

What can happen if you decide to stop and go no further? Well, you may have an experience much like Caroline had. Your refusal would be much like my refusal to start working with my dreams. I was attacked at night until I began the creative work of understanding my dreams and my inner process.

It's as if my soul knew I'd be sitting in front of clients who had little or no knowledge of things like dreams and the process of transformation. It's as if my soul knew thirty-five years ago that I'd be writing these words on these pages. The soul is not limited to time-space information; thirty-five years ago is no different from today or thirty-five years from now. Dreams and emotion are omnipresent, much like how we perceive God.

Caroline was back in my office, so I got started. We again used EMDR, targeting the fear of a recent thunderstorm that lasted close to an hour and was pretty scary even by Florida standards. I asked her if there was anything she had forgotten to put on her timeline.

"No, I don't think so," she replied.

I had no choice but to target the thunderstorm, yet I

was pretty sure Caroline's fear of thunderstorms was only the symptom, the symbolic representative of something hidden. She was on her way out of Gethsemane and into stage three, her crucifixion. The unconscious will become an ally if you honor and work with it, but deny it, and it will attack. Honor it, and it will help; deny it, and you will pay the price.

Sanford's words describe this price: "if one turns aside the demands of the creative and seeks to return to a life of unconscious obedience, his [or her] fate will be worse than that of Sodom and Gomorrah. God can be harder on those who are close to him than on those who have never known him, precisely because they may achieve something creative.[25]

In the end, this is an invitation from God who, it has been said, has a wonderful plan for each of us. It is up to us to discover it. In a way, EMDR shines a bright light on this truth and helps those who take the journey to discover their true and authentic purpose. As Sanford says, "The Kingdom is not obedience, but creativity; it is not restoration to a former primitive state from which man fell, but is reunification on a much higher level.[26]

Perhaps it is no coincidence that Christ, too, expressing his human nature, made such a human request to avoid his passion, to avoid all this pain and suffering that awaited him. Fulton Sheen states in his book *The Life of Christ*, "All men are born to live; He was born to do the Father's business, which was to die, and thereby to save."[27]

Christ, knowing that his purpose, his reality was to suffer a brutal death, and rise from the dead, still prayed to avoid it all. Yet, almost in the same breath, he surrendered to it, which is the move to stage two in the psychological process of EMDR. Most people take years, even decades to get to stage two. Christ got there in moments.

Sanford, in his book *Healing and Wholeness*, describes the process of individuation.

He says: "The individuation process is usually quite painful. It requires learning much about ourselves that we would prefer not to know, assuming the burden of our inner conflicts. Becoming whole is a dark and dangerous passage, and it is small wonder that most people avoid it if they can."[28]

He concludes, "We can even speak of individuating as a 'divine wound.' "[29]

I view my clients as being holy and near to God. They come into my office often broken and shattered, but I feel that they are special, and that, if they can recover from the wound, they will become who God wants them to be — their most authentic self. What wound can be more divine than a crucifixion?

The unconscious can behave like a petulant child or an angel from heaven. It is, however, acting in the service of the soul.

Logically, Caroline knew that her response to storms was ridiculous, but it made perfect emotional sense. More than anything else, the soul wants connection. It longs for an authentic relationship with the person, so this mysterious language of the soul must be understood and experienced.

Caroline was carrying her cross and being crucified, and I could only watch. She bravely went down a path she did not want to tread. She stayed in Gethsemane as long as she could. Then her soul had enough of Gethsemane and activated severe symptoms that would force her to reconcile her past, which she bravely did.

She stayed in this pain for twenty minutes or so without stopping. Once it subsided, she became very calm and tired. Her blouse was wet from the flood of tears that had fallen from her eyes, and snot dripped from her nose, a common sight in my office.

As I handed her a tissue, I asked, "What was that about?"

She had an encounter with what Jung would call her collective unconscious. She accessed shadow material, material that is hidden from consciousness, material that causes problems in our present life, problems that were clearly happening to her.

She tearfully admitted her truth: "My father molested me when I was six or seven. I don't know what that has to do with thunderstorms, but once I started thinking of thunderstorms, my mind went right to those memories, and I could not move away from them. They all flashed in front of my eyes; it was like I was a little girl again and the adult sitting in this chair at the same time. It was weird."

Together, we targeted the molestation for the next session, which was less intense than the previous one, after which her fear of thunderstorms disappeared for good. EMDR cured her and brought her peace, a peace she had never felt in her life.

You are probably asking yourself, what does being molested have to do with thunderstorms? I guessed that she had been molested during a thunderstorm, but she said that was not the case. Rather, her father would take her out to his sailboat parked in the back yard, telling her that he was going to work on the boat. For obvious reasons, he never did this in the rain.

She was as curious as I was, but understanding the emotional logic of the language of the unconscious is not always easy. The wonderful thing about EMDR is that we don't always have to understand *why* for the healing to occur. EMDR accesses unconscious connections. It seeks and destroys the linkage, whether we understand or not.

We did, in this case, solve the puzzle. As I said, Caroline is bright. We figured out that being molested is very much like a Florida thunderstorm. Here are the parallels:

She never knew when her father was going to come home drunk and molest her. In Florida, you never know when a thunderstorm is going to occur. They can "come out of the blue." In fact, Caroline used this cliché.

She never knew how long the molestation was going to last. In Florida, a thunderstorm can last for days, like a hurricane or tropical storm, or it can last minutes.

Caroline said that she never knew how bad it would hurt, and that she was always terrified during these episodes. Florida has tropical storms that can be very scary.

She said: "I didn't know if I was going to live. Sometimes, I feared for my life because I did not understand what was happening to me." In Florida, an average of sixty people die every year from being struck by lightning.

You can see that the unconscious created havoc in her life, but it caused her to complete what she had started. Her soul had put her in hell, forcing her to face her truth, to take up her cross, and to surrender to her darkness, much as Christ had to do. She took the journey and was now free.

The symptoms, which sometimes have to become unbearable for a client to come in for help, are great gifts. They can lead to healing and freedom for the client. The symptoms often provide clues for the initiation, those who think emotionally and symbolically, but I must say, it is not always easy to get the message that the symptoms are trying to share. EMDR is such a great tool because it gets to the mystery faster than the most skilled therapist.

With EMDR, we do not have to talk about the trauma. I just get occasional images. I jump in and out of the process quickly.

After EMDR, some people want to talk about the events, and I'm the person who bears witness to what they have endured. Usually, though, the traumas are healed, and the clients feel no need to reveal what has happened to them. I always leave it up to the person. I try to provide whatever they need to be healed, transformed and validated.

Recently, Caroline sent me a photo of herself in her cap and gown, holding her diploma with pride. She had always been interested in studying the environment, but she had thought she was too old to return to school, especially as she had children.

With the love and support of her husband, she earned a degree in environmental science, and she and her husband are considering moving to Alaska to be immersed in the nature they both love. She is on her true and authentic path. She is most certainly beginning the journey that God has planned for her — much better than watching The Weather Channel all day, fearful of a possible storm. Now, there is only sunshine and fresh air for her even on a cloudy day.

9

Instantaneous Crucifixion to Stage Three

As I have said, these stages do not always follow a nice, neat, linear path. Sometimes the process of transformation begins suddenly and unexpectedly and brings one to the gates of hell in an instant, as it did with Tony. We find him immediately in stage three: The Crucifixion.

Tony's stage three was followed by a move to stage four, entombment and loss of identity, feeling chaos and confusion, and then by a slow move to stage five, his rebirth and the beginning of his new identity, as his previous identity was dismantled and destroyed in an unexpected and violent way.

Sometimes you do not get the chance to avoid your reality (stage one). Sometimes you do not get a chance to surrender. The crucifixion is upon you without warning; the dismantling and destruction of all that you are has begun.

You may feel that life is good. You may find yourself sitting outside on your porch, with your morning coffee, looking across the front yard toward the beautiful pond that sits just beyond the tree line on your property. It's all yours. It's all perfect.

Sometimes retirement seems just as wonderful as you

imagined it would be. Sometimes you wonder why God has blessed you with such an idyllic reality to share with your wife, whom you have loved since high school. Yes, sometimes it is all perfect.

Then *POP!* A gunshot rings out. You leave your morning coffee to investigate that sound, and you find your son lying on the floor. A pool of blood is around his head, and he is making a horrible gurgling sound as he gasps for air. You are a retired fireman, an EMT, so you go into action.

You scream, "Call 911!

"I've got to stop the bleeding!

"Keep him conscious!

"I've got to keep him conscious!

"I've got to save him!

"I saved hundreds!

"I can save him!

"I have to save him!"

But sometimes, you can't save him.

"Please, God, not this time, please do not let me fail this time.

"Please let me save this one, just one last time, God, please let me save my son."

No, sometimes, you do not get a chance to avoid trouble or pretend it did not happen. Sometimes, you do not get a choice to surrender. Sometimes you just find yourself in an instant nailed up on the cross, and you wonder, *how the hell did I get up here, and how the hell do I get down?* Sometimes you don't want to come down, because sometimes death seems easier than trying to live.

A colleague referred Tony to me for EMDR. When I first met Tony, the agony on his face scared me. I had treated couples who had lost a child many times before, but none of them had looked like this. I had seen thousands of pictures of Christ in agony on the cross, but none of these images of Christ showed a grief that could compare to the agony on this man's face. I had seen and treated severely depressed people in my office plenty of times, but I had never seen anything like the tormented expression on Tony's face. I will never forget it.

I was afraid to approach him, but I gathered my courage, trying my best to hide my uneasiness, and shook his hand. It was a handshake of a man emptied.

Tony was tall and lanky. He had long blondish and grey hair. He wore old, tired jeans and worn-out running shoes. He looked like an old surfer, which he was. He was a fireman by trade, a tough guy, a man's man.

He took care of business. He talked of being a strong man who could handle anything. He said, "I used to be three hundred pounds of muscle."

I never would have guessed that. Today he was old, thin, and frail. Nevertheless, I had a sense that if someone made him angry, he would be ready to defend his honor, and he would not back down.

He was with his wife, who was petite, and not in much better shape than he was. She agreed, though, that she was doing a little better than Tony. "I have not been able to let her leave my side," he said. They had been high-school sweethearts; they'd been together forever.

Sally said: "I haven't been able to go to work since our son died. Tony needs me with him."

He knew that she would have to get back to work, but he did not know if he could bear having her out of his sight. "What if something happened to her?" he said.

I began to do what I do. I told him about EMDR. I told him that over the years I had treated eight or ten couples who had lost a child, and that EMDR had helped them enormously. I do not know if he believed me, but he was so desperate that he was willing to try anything.

I did the typical interview and set up a few sessions with Tony, all within a week. He was in bad shape, so I did not want him to wait. He had had thoughts of suicide, but he said that he would never leave his wife like that. He just wanted to see his son.

His son had been depressed most of his life. It had started at age six, and he had lived until he was thirty-three — a long life of torment. Tony and his wife had tried everything to help him, but nothing seemed to work for very long.

Tony said, "I know he just got tired of fighting this depression every day." Tony's son was a Christian, and perhaps, if thirty-three years was enough for Christ, it was enough for Tony's son.

At our second meeting, Tony did not look much better, and he was still holding on to his wife. He was not able to drive. He told me about two large tattoos he was having done on his shoulders.

He said, "You know, doc, some of James' ashes were

mixed into the ink that made these tattoos, so he is always with me now," as tears slowly moved down his cheeks.

This man loved his only son. He said, "We were best friends; we did everything together." As I said, Tony was a tough guy, a hero, but a man you should not mess with — the opposite of his son. Tony told me about James: "He was a gentle soul who loved God despite his torment."

He shared a story that created a picture of their differences:

"Doc, if someone cuts me off, or starts to tailgate me, I've been known to chase them down and confront them. If this happened when James was with me, he'd try and calm me down. I can still hear him, because he'd always say the same thing: 'Dad, let him go. Let's just relax and enjoy the drive together.'

"Regrettably, I rarely did what he asked. I would chase the drivers down and yell at them." Tony had tears rolling down his face. Then he suddenly stopped crying and smiled. I had never seen a smile on his face.

"What just happened?" I asked. "What caused you to smile just now?"

He said, "I just saw a Jeep with a surfboard pass your window."

I asked, "So that got you to smile?"

"Yea, I'm at peace on the waves."

This was good, a step toward stage five, even if only for a minute, so I said, "Do you still have a board?"

"Hell, yeah. I always have a board."

"When was the last time you were out on the ocean?"

"Not since my son died," he said. "My wife is afraid I'll get hurt, and she couldn't bear it if anything happened to me."

"Tony," I asked him, "how long have you been surfing?"

"I've been surfing my entire life."

"Have you had any accidents?"

"No, not for over thirty years," he said. "I am very careful."

"Maybe you could take a short, safe ride on moderate waves," I said. "You came to life a minute ago. Do you think you would enjoy surfing?"

"Yeah," he quickly replied, "I miss it, and I love it. I forget everything and feel so free on a wave."

He agreed to discuss the idea with his wife, and she was OK with it. With the EMDR, and the simple joy of surfing again, he began to improve.

He talked about his son. "I think James looked up to me, but, you know, he had it right, and I was wrong. He was the kind soul, and I was the tough guy." This statement showed a slight change in his thinking and a move to stage five. He was thinking of his past behavior and what his son's view of the world was like.

We continued with EMDR. These were emotionally grueling sessions. He shed a river of tears, and guys like Tony don't usually cry. I told him he had to surrender. "If you feel like crying, try to let those tears out in here."

In a few months, Tony's life began to change. He wanted his son's death to have a purpose, a purpose more than ending thirty-three years of depression and emotional torment. He started to think about how he could help people in his retirement years. He loved dogs and trained two of them to become therapy dogs. He visited nursing homes every day with them.

"You know, doc, James would be proud of me," he said. "James loved the Lord, and I'm trying. I started to go to church, and I bring happiness to these unfortunate older people who have very little joy in their lives. They light up when I come with my dogs."

Tony's life has improved. His wife is OK, but she struggles from time to time. They are slowly moving on with their lives. They can speak of the good times with their son, and they do not break down every time they see a picture of him or hear a song on the radio that reminds them of him.

Tony got down from the cross and moved through stage four, the period of chaos and confusion, the period of suspended animation, the period where your identity is lost. In an instant, Tony was no longer a father. Before that instant, he had been a strong, tough man, a proud father who loved his son. This identity died with his son.

Tony became something new — not a father, but still a husband, still a surfer, still a man's man, but a gentler man. He began to love God, and he took pride in the work he was doing with his therapy dogs.

He said: "You know, doc, my son in his death has become my mentor. He has turned me into a better person. You know, I think he's looking down on me, and he is proud of the person I am becoming. It's strange how these things work out, isn't it?"

I wasn't sure what to say, except to agree with him. I know every day is a struggle for him. I know he misses his son terribly. However, as a courageous man, he is putting one foot in front of the other every day, and he is trying to make his son proud of him every day. He is an honorable man. Many do not recover from such an event. Tony is one of my heroes.

Sometimes, as a therapist, you feel honored and privileged to accompany souls in trouble during the most horrifying periods of their life. Sometimes, as a therapist, you wonder when the day of your crucifixion will come, because you know it will come, and you hope you have half the courage and strength of people like Tony and his wife, who have made it through the deadly darkness. But they would probably both agree that it is a daily struggle.

So, what is this old self, and why do we have to change? Why do we need to discover this new self or this new way? Why do we have to go through all this trouble? Why can't we just skip all this and just keep on doing what we do?

علم

Jung said, "All true things change, and only that which changes remains true. . . . Man is placed by God in the furnace of tribulation, and like the hermetic compound he is troubled at length with all kinds of straits, divers, calamities, anxieties, until he dies to the old Adam and the flesh, and rise again as in truth a new man."[30]

In stage three and four people feel desolate and alone. "My God, My God, why have you forsaken me?"[31]

Christ said, "You must be born again to enter the kingdom of God." He also stated, "For whoever would save his life will lose it, but whoever loses his life for my sake will find it."[32] There are many interpretations of this statement, but most of his teachings can mean many things, much like the symbols our unconscious presents to us in our dreams. As I have said, symbols are not limited to time and space. Neither are Christ's words.

Jesus used simple but brilliant language when he spoke. His words can mean something to a twelve-year-old, something different to a forty-year-old, and something completely different and relevant to an eighty-year-old.

Christ understood human psychology, as well as human religion. I am a psychologist who thinks like a psychologist, but the religious parallel is striking and should not be ignored or dismissed. Christ's words have enormous religious value, but they also can be interpreted psychologically. When these two worlds are combined, the healing potential increases exponentially.

EMDR helps people become their authentic selves, the people God wants them to be. They must die. The old self must be crucified before the new self can be born. The command to be "born again" must be fulfilled. This born-again self understands the true and unique path for the person brave enough to engage in this adventure. At the end of the work, the path is unencumbered by past relationships, past tribulations, or the negative core beliefs that are a part of the old self, like Tony's "I'm a tough guy" belief.

Tony could not choose whether he would change or not. He was attacked by a horrible event, so change came to him suddenly and violently. He had to adapt or die. He chose to adapt in honor of his son.

10

Stage Four: Ready To Be Reborn
or Perhaps Not ...

Ron was an Afghanistan veteran, a hero by the looks of him. I liked Ron, an honorable young man who had struggled since returning to the states from his many tours in Afghanistan. I would have been proud to have him as a son. He was tall, lean, and all muscle. If I was in a battle, I'd want Ron there with me, but I doubted if he'd want me there with him.

He had very short hair, and he had tattoos that he talked about but that I could not see. He came for sessions directly from work, carrying what was left of a gallon of water and his backpack.

He said: "My unit was in a cave. We had orders to hold our fire. The enemy is closing in. If we don't open fire soon, we will all be slaughtered. Our commander shouts his order, 'Hold your fire,' when every cell in my body is saying, *shoot,* but I obey and hold my fire. The enemy is almost on top of us, firing at us, bullets ricocheting everywhere. Finally, we get the order, 'Fire!' We slaughter them all.

"There is blood everywhere, bone fragments, and brain

matter all around us, but I'm alive. I can't believe it — I am alive!

"The next thing I know, I'm on a stone slab surrounded by men. I am undressed down to my underwear. I'm on my knees with my hands bound behind my back.

"I'm thinking, *how the hell did I end up here?*

"Then Christ walked in and touched my shoulder. Christ said, 'Ron, get up.'

"I thought, *But I'm bound. I can't get up.* I said to Christ, 'I can't get up because I'm bound.'

"Christ touched my shoulder and said in a gentle, loving voice, 'Ron, rise.'

"Surprisingly, I was able to get up. I was not bound anymore.

"Christ looked at me and held my left arm firmly and gently, in a grip that was like no other — a grip of love, of truth, of understanding, all this with one touch. He said: 'Ron, it's OK. Ron, you're free. It's OK.'

"He looked at me, and with those God-like, piercing, loving eyes, he said again: 'Ron, it's OK. You're free.' That's it. Then the dream ended." *

---

* C.G. Jung would sometimes enter his client's dreams using active imagination to better understand their dream and the client. I had never felt a need to do this, but I did with Ron. The bold letters are from my active imagination session of his dream. Active imagination is a technique where one sits quietly, relaxes, and enters a dream one wants more information about. It is usually not someone else's dream. It is usually the dreamer's dream. We will learn more about active imagination in a later chapter.

Ron was tormented by his military experience — by what he did, by what he didn't do, and by what he thought he should or could have done. In the end, EMDR helped him a great deal, as he slowly came to terms with it all.

Ron's dream represented stages three, four, and a movement toward stage five. The dream was of destruction. Ron's old self was destroyed. Then, however, an encounter with Christ encouraged Ron to move to stage five — a rebirth. The message was clear. It was OK for Ron to move on and let go of the past. "Ron, you're alive, so live."

But to do so was not so easy for him, as he was suspended in stage four — entombment. He was struggling with his identity. He was probably conflicted, asking himself: "Shall I behave like a warrior and honor those fallen by refusing to go on with my life? Do I keep a solemnity about me in honor of my fallen brothers?"

The dream took place in a tomblike cave. Ron was a prisoner there, chained to stage four, even though he was actually free to go. He had an underground struggle in the dark, in the place of in between, a place where his warrior identity had value, and a place that had a way out. The way out, however, meant he must leave the dead and get away, get on with his life as a civilian.

Either choice was a losing one. If he got on with his civilian life, he would feel guilt about those who were lost. If he didn't get on with his civilian life, he would feel guilt about disappointing his wife and family.

Most people who come into my office are right where Ron was. They are in a lose/lose situation.

When they come into my office, I usually tell them the "Lizard and the Fire" fairy tale. It is not a happy fairy tale, like "The Sleeping Beauty" or "Beauty and the Beast," so few clients have ever heard of it, but one thing I have learned in my life and work is that there is nothing nice and neat about living on this earth. There is nothing nice and neat about this little story. When I tell it, there is an uncomfortable pause at the end. No cheers, no laughs, just an uncomfortable silence.

Ron is holding the lizard, as you will see from the fairy tale. Here it is:

The Lizard and the Fire

Once upon a time, once, before there was time, once beyond time, there was a boy, and, well, it was his time. It was time for him to go deep into the jungle with the men. The men would take him there safely, and they would teach him. They would tell him everything they knew and everything they thought he would need to know. All the wisdom of the tribe would be offered to him now, because his time had come.

They went, and they were deep into the jungle with the wild animals and the heat of the sun. The warriors would teach him about war, the hunters would teach him to hunt and track, the holy men would teach him about God, love and forgiveness, and they would all warn him about hatred and war. They would teach him how to find water and how to make a fire.

It's strange, he thought, but they taught him to weep, and to shudder, and they taught him to dance. He was surprised that the warriors would teach him how to cry. He was moved by their weeping as they told about their losses in war. They taught him that a man who cannot dance, who cannot cry, who cannot love, is not a man.

After they taught him all they had to teach him, they slowly hugged the boy one by one and left him in the jungle alone. He was to stay there for three days. The last man to leave the boy was the father. He embraced his son with a tear in his eye and gave one last piece of advice.

He said, "Son, if you see a beautiful maiden out here, do not spend the night with her, because if you do, you will surely die."

The son said, "Yes, father, but I do not think there'll be any maidens out here."

The boy did well in the jungle, because the men had taught him well. Nevertheless, at dusk, on the second evening, a beautiful maiden from a nearby village became lost and happened upon the boy. The two talked and talked for hours, as they found they had much in common. Before they knew it, it was night. This particular night was very dark. Clouds covered the sky, so there were no stars, no moon, just darkness.

The maiden said she was too afraid to go back to her village, because she would surely get lost in the darkness.

The boy said, "You can stay with me."

She agreed.

"There is one thing, though," he said, "My father told

me if I met a beautiful maiden out here in the jungle I should not spend the night with her, because I would die."

The maiden was shocked by this news, and said, "I will sleep somewhere else, because I do not want you to die."

"It can't be true," he said. "Please stay."

She stayed, and in the morning, the boy was dead.

The maiden rushed to his village and told the villagers what had happened. The tribe went into action. Some went to get the sage of the village to ask what they should do. Other villagers went to get the boy. The boy's mother wept, his father was sad, and the others in the village tried to comfort them.

The sage said: "You must build a very large fire, a fire so large that it can be seen for miles. Then, bring the boy to the fire and get me a lizard." All of this was done quickly. The fire blazed. The boy's lifeless body was set next to the fire. The entire village surrounded the fire and the maiden. The mother and the father were between the boy and the sage.

The sage said: "Here's the situation. I am going to throw the lizard in the fire. If a woman can retrieve it, the boy will return to life."

He threw the lizard in the fire, and the boy's mother immediately jumped into the fire, but the lizard ran from her, and she could not retrieve it. Then the maiden jumped in, and the lizard leaped into her hands. She gave the sage the lizard, and the boy came back to life. The villagers cheered. The mother grabbed the boy and hugged him tightly.

All cheered except for the sage. He solemnly stood there, holding on to the lizard, for he knew there was more that had to be done.

The sage said: "Young man, come here. Here is the situation. Open your hand." The young man opened his hand, and the sage gave him the lizard. "You now hold the lizard. If you set it free, your mother will die, and if you throw it into the fire, the maiden will die. The choice is yours."

You see, people who come into my office are very often holding the lizard, much like Ron, and no matter what they do, they lose. This is an adult story, because this is an adult moment. Often there is only one thing to do: pray.

Unless, of course, you remain in the avoidance stage your entire life, but that would be a life that has not been lived. You can only get to the "lizard and the fire" moment if you have loved, or cared, or tried something for a righteous reason but it all turned out badly, or if you have tried something you believed in but failed.

I remember the very first "lizard and the fire" moment that came walking into my office when I was at a large university completing my internship. The undergraduate was a bright and academically successful young woman who rarely misbehaved. She had been raised as a Catholic and strongly held those beliefs. She rarely went out with her girlfriends to party, and she never got drunk.

On one occasion, however, after her final midterm exam, she agreed to go with her friends. She went out, got drunk, had sex with a boy who had been her friend for years, got pregnant, and was now in my office, trying to decide what to do.

She only had "lizard and the fire" choices.

First, she could have an abortion, but for a Catholic this would be unforgivable, and for her it was not really an option, although she said during an early session that she actually was considering it.

"You know, Andy, I am and always have been against abortion, but now that I'm pregnant, I can see why a woman might have one. I wish I could just make this go away."

Second, she could give the child up for adoption. She fretted over this choice, even though she had already contacted a Catholic organization and received counseling and information about her choices. "I just don't know how I would feel after carrying my child to term and handing it off to another couple. I don't know if I could do that at all, but I'm considering it."

Third, she could quit school, giving up the learning that she loved and at which she was very good. She never felt confused about her career. In fact, this young woman seemed to have had her feet on the ground and her head on straight since she was six years old.

She said: "You know how people say, 'She is an old soul.' All the adults around me have said that about me my entire life." She had always known what she wanted and did what was expected of her. She had made her parents very proud, and she loved her life.

When she was in school, she was in her element. She loved school, enjoyed studying and loved God. She said many times, "Andy, I'm a lucky girl who made a single bad mistake." She didn't know if quitting school and struggling to raise a child as a single mother was the right thing to do. She didn't even know if she was capable of this enormous task. "It's as if God has given me all these gifts, and I have to set them aside to raise a child."

You see, with every choice, something dies. With abortion, her baby would die. With adoption, a piece of her soul would die. She said as much. If she raised the child, her dreams of being a pediatrician would die.

She left school, and I do not know what she chose, but she was holding the lizard.

So was Ron, and Ron's dream gives us a perfect view of where he was in this six-stage model. Dreams will sometimes represent more than one stage at a time, because the person is experiencing more than one stage at a time. Usually, however, there are clear representations of a single specific stage. The dreams reflect the reality of the present moment, whatever it might be.

Ron had done a great deal of work, but now stage four presented him with the sense of being lost and confused because his identity was changing. In the dream, he was literally in a tomb, like Christ who spent three days there, and he said in the dream in a rather confused tone, "How the hell did I get here?"

It was unexpected, because he had fought the fight and won the battle in one minute — stage three work — and then remained in stage three because he was bound, unable to move on. It looked as if he needed to do more fighting, but in fact he was free to go, a definite feature of stage five, a move to rebirth, the new life. All he needed to do was to follow Christ's instruction, "I say to you rise, pick up your bed, and go home."[33]

He had a choice here, because it was clear that he no longer had to be tormented by his past. However, being a soldier was a big part of his identity. It wasn't easy for a warrior to walk completely away from that identity.

Christ himself told him in his dream to let it go and move on to the next chapter in his life. "It's OK, Ron." This was an invitation to move to stage five, an invitation from Christ himself. This was a powerful component of the dream, as Christ pushed Ron toward his rebirth, his renewal.

Ron seemed to have completed stage three, destruction work; was trapped in stage four but unable to free himself; and was invited to stage five but not ready to make that move. Caves can be a symbol of initiation. There sure was blood and death around as well as a way out to the new life after this dream of initiation and transformation.

Ron was tearful in this session, something he did not do very often. He explained the meaning of the tattoos that were hidden from view. They were a permanent reminder of what was good, bad, or horrifying about the war he had fought, a reminder of those who had made it home and those who had not.

We were going to resolve the source of these tears in

our next EMDR session. We would try to get Ron out of stage four and into stage five. I was pleased that he had finally shared the meaning of the tattoos with me. I was pleased that Ron was ready to move on.

Ron has not, however, been back to do this last work. I don't know if he will ever do it. I do not know if he needs to do a last session. His process feels unfinished to me, but this isn't about me.

Some vets think it is dishonorable to heal and feel good while their brothers have died. Some will go only so far and then say: "I'll keep this level of pain in honor of my brothers who did not get to live their lives, doc. I can manage this. I feel good enough."

Perhaps Ron had considered doing the EMDR work on the trauma of his war experience because he did not want to disappoint me, but by completing the plan I had laid out for him, he would be betraying the memory of his comrades.

Sometimes quitting is not quitting at all. Sometimes what looks like quitting is finishing in a beautiful and perfect way for an honorable young man.

A friend asked me, "Is it hard to work with someone who doesn't get better?"

"Yeah, very hard," I replied. "Thankfully, it doesn't happen too often. I think it's probably more difficult when there is someone who I know I can help, and they won't let me help them."

Ron let me help him. He let me in for a while. He was always gracious and grateful. He never exited a session without shaking my hand firmly. He looked me in the eye and, with sincere appreciation, would say something like: "Thanks, doc, you really helped me today. I feel so much better."

Ron ended every session as if it was going to be our last, as if we might never see each other again, an occurrence that probably happened more often in a theater of war than in my quiet little office on the Florida coast.

Ron was an honorable young man who just wanted to be at peace, to be productive in his work and to love his wife. I hope he will be successful in all of these things and more. It was a great privilege for me to work with him. I think of him often, and I hope he is OK.

Sometimes the move from stage four to stage five can happen very quickly, and the process moves to an end suddenly. In this next story, the stages are very distinct and dramatic.

I met Molly at stage four, because she had done the first three stages with a different therapist. Most other therapies can take clients through the first three stages, but EMDR is needed to continue the process through to stage six.

Molly was going to transform herself, and she did. She was initially pleased with the results. No one, however, had told her about stages four, five and six. She thought that she should be finished with her therapy at stage three, much as I did before I heard the St. Elizabeth dream.

Molly told me that she now had everything she had ever wanted. She had transformed herself. "I should not be here," she said. "I should be done with this therapy stuff."

She had formerly identified herself as the "fat girl." She

was single, in her mid-thirties, a young executive following in her father's footsteps. She described her family as perfect, with a handsome brother who was, of course, the star quarterback. Her mother was attractive, petite, and wore a size zero or something. Her father was tall, well-groomed, with well-tanned skin. He was a Florida executive, and he looked it.

Then there was my client, the little "fat girl," probably a miscalculation in the conception department. "If you look at our family pictures and ask yourself who doesn't belong," she said, "well, it's obvious. It's me." To her, she had been the little fat girl in front of all the perfect people, the one who had been dropped off in the wrong family at the wrong time.

When I first saw her, she was not fat. She was thin, tall, blond, and depressed. She had recently lost more than eighty pounds. All she had ever wanted was to be skinny and fit in with her family — to be "good enough." Her dream had come true. She'd lost the weight, and now she wanted to die, and she did not know why.

"This is a dirty trick that God is playing on me," she said. "How can this be? I am supposed to be happy now."

I'd seen this happen to clients many times before, but each case is different, and each can be a bit of a mystery to figure out. At stage four, everything a client has come to therapy for is accomplished, but then trouble sometimes sets in.

Usually the client doesn't know why, and often neither do I. The beauty of EMDR is that it is a laser beam to the truth. The answer is always inside the client's head, not mine. EMDR sets the stage for the discovery of the mystery.

When I told her about EMDR, she was ready to start that minute. We set the session up and began. Things moved uneventfully for a time, and then she said, "I'm feeling afraid."

I said: "OK. Go with that." My brief comment may sound lame, but it's what we are trained to say, so as to stay out of the client's way.

She began to weep, tears pouring down her face. I waited until the tears subsided, and then I stopped the eye movement equipment. She turned to me and softly said: "I don't know who the good people are anymore, because only good people talk to fat girls. Now, everyone talks to me, and I am terrified. I don't know who to trust."

There it was. One sentence. "I don't know who the good people are any more." We were on our way out of stage four and heading to the Promised Land.

Now we knew why she was depressed, and we could get to work. Her depression lifted that day, but, now that she understood, she was anxious and uneasy for a while. Her anxiety was manageable, though, and we proceeded through the stages in a relatively short amount of time.

There you have it — a perfect example of stage four moving to stage five, with a very real danger of returning to stage one. Being the fat girl who didn't belong was easy for her. She had been doing it her whole life.

Her truth, like everyone else's, lay ahead, not behind. We navigated through these treacherous waters and this exciting new terrain. She moved through stages five and six, knowing that she could accept herself at any weight.

She discovered that there was a wonderful and healthy world out there for her. Her problem wasn't about fitting into someone else's world as much as it was about creating her own world and accepting herself. She discovered a healthy place, a place somewhere beyond the land of the "fat girl" and the "perfect family," a place that was all her own.

II

The Case for the Mystical EMDR

Remember Morton T. Kelsey? He was John's friend, a professor, Episcopal minister, and Jungian analyst at Notre Dame. In his book *Encounter with God*, he identified and described twelve spiritual rules. When a person is in the throes of an EMDR processing session, ten of these twelve rules are occurring.

Let's take a look at these ten rules to see if EMDR can actually enhance one's spiritual growth and perhaps even create an encounter with God. Perhaps EMDR is actually setting up an environment in which clients can have mystical experiences.

In EMDR, as I have said, we stop clients every so often and ask, "What are you noticing?" We don't say, "What you are feeling," because they may not be feeling anything. They may be having a body sensation, a memory, or an image, so our query is always, "What are you noticing?" On more than one occasion my client has said, "I'm talking to God."

I have also heard clients say, "I'm talking to Jesus" or "the Virgin Mary." These people are not psychotic. Rather, they seem to access a part of their psyche that the intellect and ego interferes with, so these experiences do not occur until the ego shuts down, giving clients access to this wiser self.

When EMDR works, clients gain access to a wisdom they do not typically have. EMDR helps those "holding the lizard" to figure out which bad choice is the best for them. I am amazed at the magic, or the adaptive shift, that occurs in most EMDR sessions.

One client was processing an abortion she had in college. This had happened thirty years ago. Her negative processing had brought her to a self-blame statement, "I killed it." We did not start there. I would never let someone start with such a destructive core belief, so we began with, "I did something wrong," but she immediately moved back to "I killed it" in the processing anyway.

From there she eventually got to, "My priest forgave me; that means God forgives me." Then I gave her the standard response, "Go with that," and we continued. Her response to my subsequent "What are you noticing?" was: "I was a stupid, scared little girl in college who made a mistake. If God has forgiven me, perhaps it's time I forgave myself. Apparently, I'm the only one in the universe who has not forgiven me. Maybe it's time."

She ended the session with tears, followed by a deep breath, after which she said: "I've let it go. I feel like a great weight has just left my body. I know I am forgiven."

With EMDR all of this happens in the clients' own heads. They see the truth and accept the positive shift in every cell in their body. It literally changes their psychological DNA.

She had had many people tell her to forgive herself, but it is impossible to talk people out of their emotional wounds. They let them go in their own time and in their own way. Without EMDR she might never have let go of her guilt. Confessing to a priest had not enabled her to let it go.

Talking to someone is not usually the answer. People are not healed by a "from my mouth to their ears" or vice versa moment. They have to do the processing in their own minds by accessing their soul, or what Jung calls the "collective unconscious," or, if you like, the unconscious mind, or the voice of God. EMDR takes people to a place of wisdom that they cannot access unless they are quiet as they take this journey within themselves.

It is ironic that people who would traditionally talk about their problems in therapy are being healed by keeping silent during an EMDR session. In fact, this may be the only hour that a person actually spends in silence, rather than being tethered to some distraction like a cell phone, computer, iPad, or iPod — not to mention old-fashioned distractions like television and radio.

I am a child of the industrial age, but I am by no means a digital wizard. During one of the weeks I took off from work to write this book, I lost my cell phone at the Charlotte airport, and it was not returned. I was without a cell phone for less than twenty-four hours, but it was difficult. There were people I wanted to text or call. I couldn't check emails unless I was in front of a computer. I was shocked at just how lost I was without that stupid thing.

On the other hand, it was freeing. My office had my

wife's cell phone in case of emergency, and my family had been notified to call her, so there was no real problem. I was alone, in a quiet room, writing, for about six hours. I had nothing to do except write. It was a wonderful experience.

When clients sit in my office for EMDR processing sessions, they are sitting in silence and taking a look at their darkest and most troubling memories. They have no opportunity to change the subject or to minimize the trauma. They are transported to a place where they have to feel it all one more time, but this will be the last time. After their journey, the traumatic memory will never bother them again.

Let's take a look at Kelsey's twelve spiritual rules and see if they are present in the process of EMDR.

Rule No. 1: Act as if the spiritual realm exists.

EMDR requires a complete surrender to a person's history. There is a level of "acting as if," because many of my clients say that they did not think watching these blue lights move back and forth was going to do anything, but they went along with the program. They "act as if" it is going to work. It usually does work.

During EMDR processing, clients encounter many things. As I have said, on many occasions clients have indicated that they were talking to God. Also, images appear that one might say are nothing more than fantasies, but they can have a profound effect on the clients having them.

I was working with a young woman, and I asked,

"What are you noticing now?"

"I'm talking to God," she replied.

I said: "OK. Go with that. I don't want to interrupt God." I was serious, and she was in tears at the time.

She had been struggling in her marriage and had said: "I have to love my husband. He is afraid with the economy and how he will support our family. He loves us, and he needs my love, not my criticism." Her talk with God helped her immensely with her family situation.

Such clients do not have to act as if the spiritual realm exists. They will encounter it. EMDR helps bypass the ego, quickly giving access to the collective unconscious, as Jung would say, or perhaps access to God. Either way, this process offers clients a powerful connection to something they do not have access to with their egos.

Rule No. 2: Undertake the quest with serious purpose.

EMDR must be done with a serious sense of purpose, or it will not work. It is perhaps the most serious work one can undertake, the work of the soul. Clients know it is serious business. Powerful discharges of emotion are painful but necessary for healing to occur.

This is not just a treatment. Clients are on a quest, a sacred journey, a holy, dangerous and often psychologically bloody journey with the rewards of rebirth, a resurrection and a new life of authenticity — a knowledge that they are living the lives they are meant to live and not the lives everyone else wants them to live.

Rule No. 3: Seek companionship and spiritual direction.

As I have said in the first chapter, during an EMDR processing session, I do not feel as much like a psychologist as a companion or a midwife helping the client through serious labor pains to get to the new self. There is often discussion of God and other spiritual issues, and often clients seek out their own spiritual directors, too, as Nicole did in chapter two. This rule is certainly present in the EMDR therapy.

This work cannot be done by buying an EMDR machine and doing the work on oneself. Clients cannot make their eyes move back and forth and be healed. There is an essential human to human component.

Rule No. 4: Turn toward the inner world through silence and introversion.

The idea of silence was addressed in the beginning of this chapter. There is no unnecessary talking during EMDR. Clients must surrender to the process and allow whatever happens to happen. They are instructed not to try to make anything happen, but also not to try to prevent anything from happening. They become passive vessels, ready for processing.

This is a profound move inward. It is done in silence,

except for the bi-lateral stimulation, which seems to enhance the move inward rather than to distract the clients away from their inner worlds.

Rule No. 5

Kelsey's Rule No. 5, "Learn the value of genuine fasting," is not anything I discuss with my clients. They are in the throes of battle. I want them to eat in a healthy way. Fasting is not done during EMDR work.

Rule No. 6: Learn to use the forgotten faculty of imagination.

Sometimes incorporating the EMDR bi-lateral stimulation with active imagination strategies developed by C.G. Jung helps clients dramatically. These strategies utilize the imagination in a powerful way. The use of the imagination is important in EMDR work much of the time. It is present in the understanding of dreams as well.

Rule No. 7: Keep a journal.

A journal is not mandatory, but I do encourage clients to keep one, especially a dream journal. Journaling is very important in the fourth stage of the process, at a period when internal work must be done alone. Clients must look inward at where they have been, see what it's like to have a new perspective, and decide how they are going to proceed through the next parts of their lives.

These are questions that EMDR cannot answer, nor can the therapist. Here the work must be done by the clients, with quiet, solitary looking inward to try to understand what they want the next chapters of their lives to be like.

This is a period of unknowing, a period of incubation, and a period in the womb, preparing for the new self to emerge. It is Christ's three days in hell.

During this time, journaling and dream work are very important.

Rule No. 8: Keep a record of your dreams.

I have spent a couple of decades working with my dreams and many years with my clients' dreams. Dreams offer a powerful way of getting to know your inner self. Do not ignore these nightly treasures.

People will say that they do not dream or they cannot remember their dreams. I remind them of the scientific fact that everyone dreams every ninety minutes or so when they go in and out of the REM stage of sleep. I ask clients to put notebook and pen beside their beds. If, at any point during the night, they remember their dreams, they should write a few sentences that will help them recall the dreams in the morning.

Once their notebooks are there, they are surprised at how many dreams they recall and how helpful these dreams are in understanding what stages they are in as they move through this process.

Rule No. 9: Be honest with yourself.

EMDR requires that clients surrender so that the process can take them to their truths, as we saw with Caroline, the lady with the fear of thunderstorms, who was reluctant to go where she needed to go.

There is no way for clients to do this work without a willingness to accept their truths, no matter how dark and dreadful they are. Honesty is necessary during EMDR.

Rule No. 10: Let your life manifest genuine love.

After this work is finished, clients begin to accept themselves and to love themselves. If they can't love themselves, they are incapable of loving others. Most of my clients have a core belief that they do not matter.

The belief "I don't matter" has a devastating effect on people's lives. If people do not matter, they will marry people who are selfish and happy to use them as if they do not matter. They will never say no to a request. They will do whatever anyone asks of them, because they do not matter, but everyone else does.

This is a devastating view. Our mission is to find our purpose, not to do what others tell us to do. These are lost lives, lost because those who cannot love themselves cannot love others.

Through the lens of "I don't matter," clients have no idea what they want, who they are, or what they enjoy. All they know is what other people expect of them, and they deliver that to the people in their lives.

Nevertheless, once their core belief, "I don't matter," is dismantled and changed to "I do matter," their worlds begin to change dramatically.

They cannot tolerate such treatment any more. Their worlds are open to the possibility that they can love themselves, and that they can choose people to love, people who will return their love, and who will treat them as they should be treated.

Rule No. 11: Gird yourself with persistence and courage.

As you have seen from some these stories, it takes courage to start this work, and it takes courage to finish it. The good news is that the work is transformative. It does create an authentic person, a person who sees the world clearly, who sees his or her life through a clear lens, not one clouded with past emotional wounds as a guide. For the first time, the client is free, and today's decisions are just about today with no link to the past.

Persistence is easy after the work is finished, but during the work there is a great need for courage, trust, and belief that this journey is sacred, necessary, and pleasing to God.

Rule No. 12

Kelsey's Rule No. 12, "Give generously of your material goods," has nothing to do with EMDR.

As you can see, of these twelve spiritual rules, ten are present in the transformational work that occurs in my therapy office.

12

Language of the Soul

During EMDR sessions, the therapist says two things. Every once in a while the therapist intervenes and asks, "What are you noticing?" The client is asked to share what he is noticing at that particular moment and not summarize the last three or four minutes. The skill of the therapist is important as they listen to the client's response to the query. After the response, the therapist will pick out a part of the response and say, "Go with that."

This is somewhat of an art and takes practice and experience. This is a very brief query, a quick jump into the processing and then getting out quickly, which allows the clients to stay in a mindful state of processing. There is never a breaking off to do talk therapy until the EMDR processing is over.

It is a kind of connecting the dots of the psyche. It is the skill of the therapist that comes into play here. It is a road the therapist has been down many times before, and the more experience and skill the therapist has the better it is for the client. The therapist's skill can accelerate the process or delay it. Either way, EMDR is a very forgiving process, and eventually the client gets to where they need to be. The more acutely the therapist listens, the more quickly the process will move.

I learned to listen for simple statements, because when they appear, something wonderful often happens, or something terrible that will lead to something wonderful. Jung wrote in *The Red Book*: "The soul is everywhere scholarly knowledge is not. Intuitive knowledge is superior to argument and reason."[34]

The soul speaks in "simple language," which is often a cliché that we have heard thousands of times. When I hear one in a session, I honor it and begin my exploration into its meaning. What is the soul trying to say to me, to my client? When I hear the soul's language, I say, "Go with that" with a sense of exuberance.

I also love to run with an image the client shares. If a picture says a thousand words, an image can fit into a thousand different moments in a person's life and make sense in every one of these moments. As we saw with Margaret, a rather nonsensical image of a field of petunias made a powerful impact as it reminded her of the love of her grandmother.

Clichés and images create a warp-speed connection through a person's life. Just as we saw with Nicole, "out of the blue" healed her; "out of the blue" brought her to her truth.

Images and clichés do not always appear, which is fine. It's really why I like clients to monitor their dreams during therapy, because dreams are nothing but symbols and images.

Most of the time, this process is pretty straightforward, but sometimes it is astounding. All those years of working with dreams and studying Jungian interpretations of symbols gives me a bit of a different view of these moments. I know that when I went through this transformational process myself, intellectual explanations about what I was experiencing did not help much. No, it was always rather unremarkable words that were said at the right time and in the right way that touched me deeply.

For example, I have been a fan of the band Chicago since I was thirteen years old, and I saw them perform at that age. It was a positive flash bulb moment, a moment that cannot be re-created; you only get it once. Robert Lamm, my favorite band member back then, their keyboard player and songwriter, wrote a song titled, "Goodbye." Whenever my life is going through a transition, which is always difficult, I have a Robert Lamm dream. We are usually in a church. He doesn't say much, except at the end, he says, "Goodbye" and leaves. I have had this same transition dream for forty years at pivotal times in my life. It is a rather unremarkable phrase, yet it means so much to me. The line is simple, yet brilliant, and if you're going through a transition, it kind of hits the nail right on the head. In the end it simply says, "goodbye."

This is the essence of transition; it's about moving from one thing to another. You must say goodbye to the old in order to transition to the new. Ironically, on that same album there is a song titled, "All Is Well." I usually have a dream related to this song after the transition is complete and I have settled into the new life. After decades of working with my dreams, much of my dream material is very familiar.

My clients are almost without exception doing this exact thing. They are in transition.

My ears perk up when I hear something that comes from that higher self that speaks with such simple brilliance. When I hear the simple language of the soul I become very focused on what comes next. It is always astounding to be present for these moments with my clients.

In the next chapter, you will read about my client who had to "lie down in the darkness." This phrase had a profound meaning for her, as you will see. She still carries those words with her and feels they have a comforting power beyond anything I could have said to her. This simple language of the soul is often something that we have heard thousands of times and thought nothing of it. When these words, however, present themselves in the midst of an EMDR session, I honor them and try to foster my client's exploration to an experience of these words. The beauty of using EMDR is that it takes the person where they need to go. Primarily, I have to just stay out of the way.

I have counseled a few brilliant physicians over the years, and when they get into this mindful state of processing, far away from the incredible intellectual power they possess, they too will utter simple clichés to be relieved of their burden. It is a wondrous thing to watch. Emotional issues cannot be resolved with intellect. If that was possible, these brilliant physicians, both men and women, would have solved their problem in minutes. Intellect is of no use when it comes to healing emotional wounds.

One client was terrified of palmetto bugs, and as she described her last encounter with a bug, she stated, "I don't like uninvited touching." Huh? What did she just say? I have heard a lot of ways to describe an encounter with an insect, but to describe it as "uninvited touching," well, that was a new one on me. I was pretty sure her unconscious was letting me know that this fear was not about a bug. I suspected she had experienced some uninvited touching in her life, and it wasn't from a bug. I was right.

Another client came into my office and said to me, "Andy, I am ready to get down in the dirt and do this work."

I questioned, "What did you say?"

"I'm ready to get down in the dirt."

Hmm. I never heard anyone describe starting therapy with that statement. That is the soul talking. I remembered that statement, because I knew that phrase was going to lead her to where she needed to go.

The clients, however, have to make the discovery on their own. I keep quiet when I hear these statements but guide them to this material if I can, usually in their response to the query, "What are you noticing?" I'm hoping they'll notice something related to that statement during EMDR processing. The client has to make the discovery in their own way and in their own time, but I can help.

Turns out my intuition was right about the down in the dirt statement, which led directly to one of the things she hated about her father. Apparently, her father had a beautiful flower bed in his backyard when she was growing up that he took great pride in. She said: "It was quite the sight. Clearly he loved those stupid fucking flowers more than he loved me. He couldn't give me the time of day, but he'd spend every spare moment with these stupid flowers."

We targeted the image of her father working hard in "the fucking flower bed" during an EMDR session paired with the core belief, "I don't matter." The getting down in the dirt statement led to the flower bed, and all the anger and resentment she had inside toward her dad poured out in a powerfully emotional session. She was furious at the image of him kneeling in the dirt, caring for his flowers, all the love and caring he showered on that garden, leaving little for her. This led to a review at the speed of thought of her entire life flashing before her eyes as it related to his total neglect and disregard for her.

This EMDR session ended beautifully and humorously. When EMDR gets you to be able to laugh at a tragic childhood, we have succeeded. The anger and tears began to turn to laughter and smiles. I queried, "What are you noticing?"

She stated: "These last few minutes were fun. I got into a giant bulldozer, a bright pink one. I had on a pink hard hat and pink overalls. Pink for the power of the female, and I bulldozed the shit out of that stupid fucking flower bed, and then I demolished the entire house, dug a big hole and buried it all. I left it desolated and deserted. A desert in the middle of a Cleveland suburb. A perfect symbol of all he had given me — nothing!"

Nicole, terrified of panic attacks, said, "out of the blue"

to describe her father's unpredictable abusive behavior, which connected to the present problem of panic attacks, which she said also "come out of the blue." Once the cliché was uttered and experienced in her soul, she was healed. She did not need any theoretical explanation to help her understand why she was having these panic attacks. All she needed was EMDR to allow her soul to speak, soothe, and heal, which it did with an old, tired cliché. The soul loves clichés.

Sometimes it's not a cliché, but rather an unremarkable phrase that doesn't quite fit into the present context, but certainly is meaningful and fits in better somewhere else.

Jung also described words that make the distinction between "sense and non-sense," or that meaning requires absurdity and absurdity requires meaning and their relationship to what he calls the "supreme meaning."[35] It is rare to hear a statement that might be described as "sense and non-sense." I was working with a client whose voice did not matter in her house growing up. She had no voice and learned to be invisible and quiet. During EMDR she experienced an image of a beautiful ornate box. When she opened the box in this session she said, "The box doesn't have anything in it, but it's not empty." Huh? How can it be empty and not empty at the same time?

She explained: "It is filled with the most beautiful thing, the only thing I ever needed. It's filled with air. To have a voice, all you need to do is to move air. The box contains all I need; I just need to start moving air."

She did exactly that in her life. She is now a counselor, and people listen to the air she's moving. She leads workshops and retreats, again where people listen to her every word.

Another client reported becoming angry and anxious when she entered a store to shop for clothes. In an EMDR session targeting this feeling, she said, "I get so angry when *they don't have what I need.*" She was the grown daughter of abusively neglectful parents from which she *never got what she needed.* When the store failed her it connected to all the anger she felt toward her neglectful parents. She used EMDR to process these traumas by going with, "they don't have what I need." It ended her anxiety and fear of going shopping, and it linked and processed hundreds of memories of neglect caused by her parents. Fortunately, this transformation happens at the speed of thought.

One of the most meaningful statements came to me in the period when you're almost asleep, that place before sleep but not really awake. While in that state, a line came to me: "Listen to the light of the dead." This statement foreshadowed a dream I was to have a year so later, after I got engaged to my wife.

In the dream, my wife was sleeping in my childhood bed. I was standing in the room, which was filled with different size round light bulbs — large ones and small ones — all floating in the air and providing no light, even though they were on. Then her deceased father appeared dressed as a warrior and drew a fiery sword blazing with white light, sounding like a heavenly torch or something. The room was immediately filled with blinding light, and he said, "Here, you're going to need this."

The dream ended. At this time her father had been dead for a few years, and he brought me a light. This dream was so important that my psyche wanted to notify me that an important dream was coming my way. I was to *listen to the light of the dead.* The fiery sword presented by my dead father-in-law. It seemed like he was giving me his blessing to marry his daughter, but this dream meant so much more than that. Dreams are not limited to time, space, and a single meaning.

There is a time in this process where battles must be waged against the old self. This is the internal battle, but also, there is a battle that must be waged out in the world. When we change our internal view of the world, the world resists. As Christ said, "A prophet is not without honor, except in his hometown." In Nazareth, he was just the son of a carpenter. He could work no miracles in that town when he returned. No one there bought that he was a prophet, and certainly not the messiah. People want us to remain who we are. When we change, there is usually some conflict that has to be managed. Often we have to leave.

13

Stage Four: Turning Inward

In this chapter I will emphasize the seriousness of stage four work. I will also discuss the tools necessary to navigate these treacherous internal waters. These tools are valuable adjuncts to the EMDR work. They are valuable even if you are not using EMDR, but with EMDR, their power increases exponentially.

The journal is the anchoring tool for this process. It is the most precious tool for this work. Once the old personality is dismantled in stage three, removal of the old symptoms almost complete, clients must move through stage four, the loss of identity. They must figure out what the next chapters of their lives are going to be. This is a period of shutting down, of pulling away. It is a period of creativity and solitude. The clients' work must be done alone, with journals, the use of dreams, and active imagination. The therapist can do little to help. This period is really an internal encounter that is done in solitude regularly.

Jung talks about "the desert." This is a common symbol for change or for confusion. The Jewish people were lost in the desert for forty years. Christ went into the desert for forty days to fast and pray before beginning his mission, before beginning the New Way. Jung, in his *Red Book,* writes about a period of retreating from his fellow men and disengaging from them as a pathway to his soul.

"He says that by turning himself away from men and things he became wholly identified with his thoughts, and then found that he needed to further detach himself from them. In the process his soul became a virtual desert, and by turning his creative energy toward the desert, he found that his soul would green and bear 'wonderful fruit.' "[36]

He also warns: "One will be tempted to, but must refrain from, making an early return to the world of things, men, and thoughts. Only after one has discovered one's soul can one live in harmony with men, thoughts, and things, and avoid being their slave or fool."[37]

This truth is easily understood in the context of a negative core belief, such as, "I don't matter." As we have discussed earlier, when this core belief is driving your world, unconsciously you will place everyone's needs before yours. Without insight and understanding of this internal reality, you are a slave and a fool to others. Others will take complete advantage of you unless you change that belief and allow yourself to say and believe that you matter.

I have found that my clients who resist the work of stage four, distracting themselves from their inward journeys, become ill or injured. These problems are not life-threatening, but they are serious enough to require a period of convalescence.

This is no joke. I have a list of about twenty clients who resisted, and all ended up getting so badly hurt or ill that they had to recuperate in their homes for weeks or longer. These clients were often healthy and fit. This is serious stuff, and once you start this process, your unconscious does not want you to stop.

The first client who became injured — before I had identified the six stages — was a middle-aged woman with a demanding and important job. She had always handled the pressure well. She was an excellent client and had done dedicated EMDR work. She had made a great deal of progress. One day, while she was in stage four and resisting this internal work, she showed up for an appointment wearing a neck brace and in noticeable pain.

I asked, "What happened to your neck?"

She replied, "Do you know how you said I should try to record my dreams?"

"Yes, of course I remember." I wondered, what *on earth does recording a dream have to do with a neck brace?*

"You know how you have been asking me to record my dreams, but I have been resisting?"

"Yes, I know."

"Well, I had such a startling dream a few days ago that it caused me to sit up as if possessed by something with such force that I have whiplash. I can't work for the next two weeks."

I had never heard of such a thing. It really surprised me, but the next two weeks were very productive for her. She described herself as a woman possessed, allowing herself to explore her inner world. I asked what the dream was about, but she had absolutely no recollection of the dream.

She told her story: "All I did was smoke cigarettes and write in my journals. I filled three notebooks. It was like the quiet house and my inability to move opened up the floodgates to my inner world. It's like what you have been telling me to do, but of course I never really believed you. What does writing in a journal have to do with anything, and how can that boring activity help me with anything? Boy, was I wrong!"

This was really her final step. She had figured it all out — where she had been and why, and where she wanted to go and how. She knew what she wanted the next chapter of her life to be like. She came to a powerfully comfortable place of self-acceptance and quickly moved to stages five and six. Our work together ended shortly after her period of stage four introversion: time in the tomb. She shut down, moved inward, and got on with her new life, her authentic transformed self.

Another client who resisted this internal exploration twisted her knee getting out of the shower. She, too, had to stay home from work. A third ended up with pneumonia. A fourth had a back injury from lifting something that was not particularly heavy. He just moved in an awkward position and hurt himself.

Then there was the man who ended up with a mini-stroke. He, too, had to take time off from work. It wasn't very serious, and he made a full recovery, but he spent time alone doing the inner work. Another fellow injured his Achilles heel while walking on the beach. I can go on and on about the injuries that occur when a person resists doing the internal solitary stage four work.

I recently was listening to a radio show. The host was interviewing a man who counsels people who go into religious communities. He also described this phenomenon of his clients getting sick at a particular stage in their religious development. This is not as unusual as it might seem. There is a part of each one of us that wants us to be transformed, to be free of our history, so we are able to be who we are supposed to be and do what we are supposed to do. This part often competes with the self we have always been, the self that wants no part of change.

Stage four requires a voluntary move to this essential inner exploration. It is understandable that clients resist this inner work, because stage four can be very uncomfortable. As Jung warns, people do not want to stay in the desert long enough. It is perhaps the holiest of periods, where one connects to the ancient wisdom of symbols and images. There are no iPads, cellphones, or computers in this work that can help you. These things can only distract you. This work requires paper, pen, solitude, and contemplation. If one meditates, all the better, and if one prays, better yet.

The use of the imagination is important here. Jung developed a strategy where one goes back into a dream and actively engages the dream by talking to the characters in the dream or questioning why a particular object is present in the dream. This may sound strange, because we rarely use our imagination in creative ways. This is a period of creativity.

The client below did not expand on a dream; instead,

she wanted to talk to the depression. Once she started, she was given an image of the depression. It was a black, heavy blanket that covered her entire body.

Below is an active imagination session enhanced by the bilateral stimulation of EMDR done by this client. She is the client I spoke of early who discovered the comfort of the phrase "lying down in the darkness." She was struggling in stage four with her loss of identity. Her depression was more intense after she had completed her stage three work. She was very tearful in this session, her face showing severe agony as she sat with her eyes closed, holding the tactile paddles in her hands and wearing the headphones.

Then suddenly the tears stopped, and she looked as if she was listening intently to someone. That "someone" was her inner voice, who she later said was God. Here is the exchange between her and her inner voice:

> **Client:** I can't see the light. I can't see anything with this blanket covering me. It is totally black and dark.
>
> **Inner Voice:** It's not like last time. There's nothing to fear. I am always with you. You don't believe it. Believe that I am with you.
>
> **Client:** I am afraid. I am filled with fear, afraid that it will be like last time. [Last time refers to: Twenty years ago she had been hospitalized because of a terrible bout with depression.]
>
> **Inner Voice:** Do not fight. You must learn to surrender, let go, and trust. That's why you're here

with Andy, right? To let go. He cannot do it for you. You must do it.

Client: I know, but I'm afraid. I do not know how.

Inner Voice: I will tell you how. Lie down and rest in the darkness. I am with you. I am keeping you safe while you rest.

Client: OK. I will try and stop fighting. I will surrender.

Inner Voice: This will end soon, and when it does, it will be sudden and beautiful. You will feel it immediately. You will know that I am telling you the truth. When the blanket is lifted and you come into the light, you will remember this. You will know I tell the truth and that I am always with you.

Client: OK. Thank you. I feel better, and I know I need rest. I know I have to stop fighting, because I have no more fight in me.

Inner Voice: My son set the example. He never fought. He surrendered. It is the way. Yet few have the courage or understand how to surrender. Few know how to trust in me.

Client: I know. I feel better already. I feel better to trust you and rest. I do need rest. Now the darkness feels like a friend, not an enemy. Thank you.

Inner Voice: You're welcome. Remember, trust and let go.

This is an example of active imagination. She took her

image of the depression that she was experiencing and began to speak to it. She felt hopeless before the above encounter, but hopeful after it. Active imagination is a powerful process, and when it is enhanced by the bilateral stimulation, it often works very fast.

A year later, she continued to struggle in stage four with multiple health problems that were not related to stage four. Her goal at the beginning of treatment had been to prepare for retirement, which in and of itself is a loss of identity for a professional.

She was an organized "Type A" person who always had a plan. Small things out of place bothered her; she was detail oriented with a sharp and keen perception of things. She was trying to let go of planning and sweating the small stuff. She said, "I know I have to let go of this way of living."

After a year of struggle, she confided in me that she loved that statement from the active imagination session. "When I had bouts of chronic fatigue," she said, "the voice said to 'just lie down and rest in the darkness and let me comfort you.' This meant the world to me in those episodes." She also stated, without realizing it, that everything she came to see me for was accomplished. If you will remember, however, one must do this journey without intention. Sometimes it doesn't work out exactly as planned.

She said: "You know, Andy, I was just telling Theresa, your office manager, that I never know how I'm going to feel from day to day. Some days I can get out of bed, and other days I cannot."

My office manager had said, "Wow, it must be really

hard to plan anything."

My client replied: "It is impossible to plan. I don't plan. I live my life one day at a time, sometimes one moment at a time. I have learned to accept this way of life and, actually, I am enjoying my life more."

Her stage four illness gave her what she needed to have — an unplanned retirement, just enjoying one day at a time with no agenda, no place to go, no place to be unless she was able to make the effort. Her active imagination session of a year ago had foretold this reality. "Lie down in the darkness, and I will comfort you."

She was a brave client who had the courage to enter into the work without intention.

So you see that this inner connection with the self is essential. It would not have worked to tell her what to do, because believe me, I tried. I just provided the method, the portal that would give her access to this inner wisdom, to this inner connection. She did not intellectually or cognitively know what she needed. We had to bypass her ego and intellect to get to the Self, because that's where the knowledge resides. We all possess this inner source of knowing, but we are rarely ever still enough to hear that quiet voice.

In today's digitally plagued world, it is frightening how little of this kind of work is being done, even in the schools of psychology and houses of religion. So little introspection in churches, just a lot of guitars and drums and singing and shaking. You will not find your personal God there. Yet, when people come into my office and find themselves quite alone in their own psyche during EMDR sessions, it is clear that they have had a great longing for such an experience, the experience of being alone with the Self. There is no singing or talking, there is no music, there is only silence and a chance to encounter themselves, their soul, or the voice of their God.

Alan Bloom wrote a book back in the 1980s called *The Closing of the American Mind.* Do you remember what the 1980s were like? There was no Internet, no cell phones, and few personal computers. Not everyone had a VCR, and the CD was just becoming a reality. It was a much simpler and slower world. Yet even back then, distractions were plentiful. Yes, even then, this problem existed. Imagine how much worse the problem is today and will be tomorrow?

Alan Bloom wrote: "Students have a clear idea what a perfect body is and pursue it incessantly. But deprived of literary guidance, they do not know what a perfect soul is. In fact, they do not even imagine such a thing exists."[38]

As we saw with my "lie down in the darkness" client, active imagination can be enhanced with bilateral stimulation. This process is very powerful and effective without the bilateral stimulation — something Jungian therapists have known since Dr. Jung graduated his first class of analysts. It is even more powerful and more accelerated when combined with the bilateral stimulation of EMDR.

So we have discussed the value of active imagination. Now let's take a look at synchronicity and how this might help one move through these stages. I am always on the lookout for the synchronistic event, because if one does not look, one will not see. These events go unnoticed if dreams are not attended to and written down. One must be aware of the inner workings of their own psyche to have these experiences. They are very powerful when they occur, but one cannot see them without an internal awareness. If you do not know what your dream symbols and themes are, then they cannot link to the outside world. You will not notice it. Hence the need to attend to one's dreams.

Here's a wonderful example of a synchronistic story. Marty was a fellow classmate of mine in graduate school. We became fast friends because we were somewhere in mid-life, going back to school to get our doctorates. He had a Master of Science degree in psychology and had worked in the field of psychology for years. I played piano and read about psychology for years. He was a cognitive behavioral therapist (CBT). He believed in that method, worked from that model, because he felt it had served him well. He thought dreams were silly, although he was always respectful of my view of things, as I was of his. We never debated the issue. We were really very supportive in our approach with each other. All these years later, he is the only person with whom I keep in contact from graduate school.

On one particular day, Marty and I were jogging along the beach, a regular habit of ours in those years. Before we started our run, he said, "Hey, Andy, I had a dream last night."

I said, "Oh, really, Mr. CBT had a dream." I said it with a little sarcasm and surprise. In the dream, Marty was with a good friend of his who had died when they were in high school. He had been Marty's very best friend, and Marty said that he still missed him sometimes.

In this dream, the two were looking through some old boxes and noticed that the boxes were filled with books, priceless first-edition copies of classic works of literature. Marty's friend seemed to be searching desperately for something specific, and then he got excited because he found it. He reached deep down into one of the boxes, pulled out a book, and handed it to Marty, saying: "Here it is. This is the one you'll need." The friend handed Marty a Winnie-the-Pooh book, and the dream ended.

He said he had never read a Winnie-the-Pooh book or watched a Winnie-the-Pooh cartoon. In a way, this dream confirmed Marty's suspicion that dreams were nonsense, except for the fact that he could not stop thinking about the dream or his deceased friend. Again, the soul speaks simply. It was not the great volumes of literature; no, what he needed was a book of cartoons.

He asked me what I made of that dream.

I said: "Beats me. I'm no expert on Winnie-the-Pooh, either. It's a pretty cool dream, though."

I took a gratuitous stab in the dark and said: "Maybe we shouldn't take all this graduate school stuff so seriously. Maybe it's not the priceless thing we think it is. Maybe the important thing is the simple, wiser things. Isn't Winnie-the-Pooh some kind of cartoon philosopher?" Marty did not understand this dream but thought my comment was helpful. I told him to let it sink in and think about it later. It's your dream, not mine. You'll figure it out if you want.

After the run on the beach, Marty and I walked back to the car. As Marty approached the car, he stepped on a ragged-looking solid red playing card that had been left on the ground. For some unknown reason, he picked up the tattered card and was startled to discover that the other side of this card had a picture of Winnie-the-Pooh on it. We were both shocked by this.

I exclaimed: "Wow! It's synchronicity, dude. You just had a synchronistic event. Don't throw that card away. I'd go have it framed if I were you. Looks like your friend might be watching out for you." He agreed. Even Marty, the cognitive therapist, was a bit shaken by this event. A few months later, Marty and I were off on our internship year, the final step to earn our doctorates. He was in Oregon, and I remained in Florida to be close to my family.

He said: "Andy, you're not going to believe this. One of my first meetings here at my internship site, a woman asked if I wanted a cup of coffee, and I said sure. She brought my coffee in a red cup, but she set it down with the handle on the wrong side. When I turned the cup around so the cup handle would be on my right side, guess what I saw on the cup?"

"I don't know, what?"

"When I turned the cup around, my old friend Winnie-the-Pooh was staring right at me. I think you might be right; I feel like my old, dear friend is still looking out for me. I felt as if I was connected to the universe in a wondrous way in that moment. I'm a scientist. I do not think such thoughts, but it makes sense to me. This does not feel like an ordinary coincidence; it feels like an extraordinary one. That was the sweetest cup of coffee I ever had. Not a bad way to start off my internship."

Marty's experience is an example of synchronicity. At first it may appear meaningless — it's just a dream — but the subsequent coincidence can create a change in our perspective of the world. Marty's example began with a dream, went to the discovery of a tattered card on the street, and ended with a cup of coffee. His view of his inner world began to expand. He was now open to the wonder and mystery of the human psyche; he had a new respect for dreams.

If Marty had not paid attention to his dream on that particular night, he would not have remembered the Winnie-the-Pooh dream, nor would he have ever noticed the significance of the card that he saw in the parking lot. If he had not noticed the card, he would not have noticed the significance of the coffee cup. This transforming experience would not have happened. All of these experiences begin and end with the nurturing of a relationship with your inner world.

Here is another example that happened to me as much deliberation was being taken before setting out to write this book. There were these discouraging inner voices in my head before I set out to write this book. Thoughts that were saying things internally, like, "Does the world really need another book?" "Does anyone really care what I think about anything?" My old negative core belief, "I'm not good enough," also began to reveal itself again. For a long time, I balked at the idea of writing this book. After all, writing a book is a lot of work; it takes a lot of time, and it often leads to nothing but a big fat manuscript sitting in some drawer in your desk.

It was important for me to be sure my decision was not being driven by my negative core belief, so I called my EMDR therapist and did some EMDR around this issue to clear out some old remaining links to the negative belief. This was helpful, because it seems there was some residual material linked to the "I'm not good enough" belief. After that work, I decided with a clear head and heart to proceed.

Around this time, I had just finished reading a book by Robert A. Johnson, titled *Balancing Heaven and Earth.* In it, he says that he has come to trust that whatever he needs at a particular time will show up. He calls these events "slender threads" that are always working on our behalf. In reading his wonderful biography, he makes quite a case for this reality. I, too, am working at trusting the slender threads.[39]

A day after I read this page of Johnson's book, the following event happened to me: a slender thread encounter from no one other than my old dear friend, John, with whom I have been out of touch these past few years. I do not think I've seen him in decades. I do not remember the last time I saw him in person. We used to get together in our hometown around the holidays, but his parents are deceased, and he has no family in our hometown, and I no longer live there either. So life's circumstances have made it difficult to get together.

Around Christmas, I was struggling with the title and content of this manuscript. There was a distinct Christian parallel to the psychological six-stage process, and that was a part of the new view. I was confident in this parallel, but I was wondering if other religions had similar stages. Does this psychological model only parallel Christianity (that might make sense in that psychology is a creation of the west, and Christianity is a very western religion), or does this six-stage model fit other religions? The problem: I am not a religious scholar, nor do I want to become one, although I am not opposed to researching this notion more.

Magically and unexpectedly, John, who invited me to work with my dreams all those years ago, sent me a book titled, *Thomas Merton and Sufism: The Untold Story*. Yes, this book arrived, you guessed it, "out of the blue." Ironically, he had never read the book but knew I was a big fan of Merton, and recently he had been diligently studying Sufism. He felt it would be a good book for me to learn about what he was doing spiritually, delivered by a Christian writer whom I respected and admired. He was right. It arrived a few days before Christmas as a gift for me. The provocative aspect here is that I had not spoken to him in years. We had exchanged emails a few times with rare phone conversations as of late. We had not exchanged Christmas gifts in decades. He did not know I might be setting out to write this book. Who better to send the perfect encouraging book to move me forward in this endeavor? A slender thread arrived at my doorstep by my friend John, whose impact is not really slender, more like a major artery. But the arrival of this book was a synchronistic event. It silenced my inner doubter, and I proceeded with the project.

So here we go again with, you know, my old friend, "out of the blue": A gift from John comes to my door by Merton on Sufism. A Christian discussing the Islamic mystical practice of Sufism. I couldn't put this book down. Yes, it described stages of the spiritual practice of Sufism that very closely parallel the Christian model. That exploration is for another book. It was exactly what I needed to help me move forward in my thinking about this manuscript.

This book gave me the confidence to proceed. The process became more and more important and was reinforced with every subsequent client that went through this six-stage process. Additionally, clients' dreams and imagination work continued to clearly fall into these stages.

Early on, many clients do the usual dance minimizing their traumatic past. When I hear this, I often go to the images of Gethsemane in my mind, and it occurred to me that this place where Christ was praying for a get-out-of-jail card was exactly what many of my clients experienced. Avoidance is, without a doubt, the first stage in this process. They had no interest in returning to their traumatic past, not even for a second. They were in their own Gethsemane; they wanted out but were not willing to take the dark road. They wanted to find a way around, not through. I wish there was another way, but there is not.

Somehow this six-stage idea and all its spiritual implications, as well as psychological implications, was mine to foster, share, and develop. It is a bit scary, and that is why I ignored and refused to accept this as material for a book. I said to myself, "You cannot think like this: You're a psychologist, a scientific-practitioner, not a theologian." After re-reading some of the books I read long ago that compared a psychological experience to a religious experience, I realized I had stopped thinking like a scientist years ago. This more spiritual view had always been part of me, I just did not know it. Now I began to see its reality. I began accepting it, and my clients were doing better than ever.

They had the six-stage model to hold on to. It gave them hope. They could see that they had made progress and knew exactly where they were in the process. It defeats the language of depression that says: "You're never going to get better. You're always going to feel like this." The road map tells the truth and counteracts the lies that depression's insidious inner voice screams.

This view seemed to be accurate and extremely beneficial to my clients. As these ideas came to life in my writing, my clients were sharing dreams and life experiences that solidified and supported my observations.

These mysterious events that my clients experienced, that I have shared, are about developing a relationship with the unconscious, with the self, with one's soul. They are not about giving you information about your life. If one engages this inner life, then life decisions become clearer, because you have a more clear idea who you are and what makes you tick.

The most significant effect of Marty's synchronistic event was that he no longer viewed science and empirical evidence as the only relevant experiences. He encountered mystery, wonder, and the unknown. His view of the world was dramatically expanded — by Winnie-the-Pooh, no less — another one of those "sense and nonsense moments" I spoke of in an earlier chapter. Synchronistic experiences are not always this clear or clean, but they often facilitate change.

We miss these moments if we do not take time to learn this inner language. The synchronistic event is a passive experience. You cannot force an experience like Marty's, but you can create an environment that will increase the odds that such an event will occur. That is attending to your inner life.

The active component of this work is sowing the seeds that will create a rich synchronistic soil—an environment that fosters these types of experiences. Here you take an active role in this part of the process. It requires the creation of solitude, sacredness, and ritual. It requires some connection to the inner dreamer.

Today the popular word is "mindfulness." Many books have been written about this word. For my clients, they need do nothing to find this mindful state of processing except surrender to the EMDR process. EMDR creates a mindful state of processing in seconds, often followed by profound healing. The bilateral stimulation work exposes the rich material for the psyche to continue mindful processing, and contemplative work can be done away from my office. This mindful work is essential and not difficult once the EMDR work exposes the important material, what Jung calls the *Prima Materia*.

14

Dream Work Through the Stages

*"Dream while you're awake
and be awake while you dream."*
— *Michael Thorn, my old friend*

Dream work is needed to facilitate the movement out of stage four to stage five. You cannot get to where you're going until you figure out where you want to go.

Dreams can be complex with many interpretations. If you ever read some of Carl Jung's interpretations of dreams, you get the idea of how vast his knowledge was and how endless some interpretations can be. In my six-stage model, dreams are distilled down to manageable and easy-to-understand events. They are snapshots of where you are in the process.

So here is our new model of the dream. It is the dreams in six stages: a six-stage movement from avoidance to surrender, to dismantling, to confusion, to rebirth, and finally to renewal. Each stage is clearly reflected in the dreams. Let's look at the common symbols and themes of dreams that occur in each stage.

It is amazing how similar the dreams are when my

clients move through these six stages of transformation. First, the dreams of stage one are *avoidance* dreams. You might guess what the themes are in this stage. They are those dreams where you are running but can't get away. You feel like you're falling but wake before you fall. You're being chased by something but can't run very fast. If you think the theme of the dream is to get away, *to avoid,* then welcome to stage one. People who avoid this work for decades will often report a recurring avoidance-themed dream when I ask them about their dreams.

When people come to my office, they are usually out of this stage. I do not hear many of these dreams unless they are hiding something or they are unaware that an event has significance in their work with me and therefore choose not to mention it. It doesn't matter; EMDR seeks and finds the truth. The move to stage two and three is under way quickly. You cannot do EMDR without surrendering; it will not work without surrendering to it. You must allow whatever is going to happen to happen.

Stage two and three dreams are about death and destruction. There is a killing of the old self. A crucifixion is under way, and the dreams reflect this reality. People have shared dreams of dead babies half-buried in the ground, or houses being flooded, burned down, or destroyed in a storm. It is not unusual for the dreamer to see people dying of some illness, and sometimes they themselves are dying.

One client recently provided a dream that was like an overture to an opera or musical. Almost all six stages were included in her initial dream after only one or two meetings.

As I have said, one can be in more than one stage at any given moment.

She dreamed she was giving birth. (This confused me, because birth dreams do not come along until stage five, but she was just starting.) The nurse took the baby and said everything's going to be OK. Then she reported that the baby died. (OK, now this dream was making sense to me.) Then she ran outside because she was so upset. She found herself on the edge of a lake with a large beast lying down, a giant reindeer-like animal who was her friend. It, too, was lying down next to the lake, dying. She said that there were signs posted around the lake that said, "NO SWIMMING." The dream was letting her know there was going to be death in the process. It was also letting her know that this was a no-fun-and-games endeavor. She did not come to the lake to play.

Lake and water often represent the unconscious mind, calm on the outside but filled with life hidden below the surface. The dream reflects that at one point she will give birth to a baby and it will be OK, but not yet. The beast must die for the rebirth to begin. She will have to enter the dangerous waters of the unconscious but not to swim and have fun; no, to see the darkness that lies beneath the surface. Beneath the surface is beauty, life, but also danger.

These death dreams of stage three often alarm clients, but I reassure them and tell them this is a good dream, because in our work together, we are destroying your old psychological self. In a sense, we are killing an old part of you, and that old self is dying. This is reflected in the dreams. Sometimes clients will be behind some large scary wall that they can't get beyond, but they know there is a paradise on the other side. Some people find themselves in a winter scene freezing to death with a view of the tropical paradise just over the horizon, but they can't get there.

Another common dream is when clients report that they are on a small life raft in the middle of a terrible storm and in the middle of a large, scary body of water — in the middle — the place where it's just as difficult to go forward as it is to go back. Or sometimes they are on a very high bridge that is almost ready to fall apart, but they are in the middle of it and have to make it to the other side.

Sometimes the symbols are so obvious, they are laughable. In these dreams, the client reports having other people's baggage in their car, and the car cannot move until the bags are taken out of the car. They have to decide what to do with the baggage. They have to get rid of their baggage. The inner dreamer cannot get much clearer than that symbolism.

Stage four dreams are like the one we heard earlier with Barbara, the Saint Elizabeth dream. The clients in this stage are usually lost, unsure of where they are going or where they came from. Sometimes she does not even know her own name. It represents uncertainty and a stillness, but sometimes it represents urgency. I have had a number of clients who enter a public restroom in their dream only to find all the stalls are being used or they are all broken. They need to use the restroom quickly and urgently, so they will say something to me like, "Yeah, in that dream I had to go really bad, but *I did not know where to go.*" This simple phrase represents their reality. All of these dreams are preparing for the birth. This is the dream that gives a glimpse of the new way to stage five, to the rebirth.

Stage five dreams are wonderful, and when I begin to hear them, I know the worst is over for the client. Stage five brings the new life. These dreams often represent pregnancy dreams or even delivering a child in the dream. I even had a few men who dreamt that they were pregnant and giving birth to a child. This made them a bit uneasy, but once I explained what was happening, they were encouraged by it. Perhaps the most beautiful dream image that I had heard in stage five was when one of my clients was making her way to stage five. This was the dream she shared but did not really understand.

"I'm walking along a red clay dirt road like they have in Georgia, and I see a corn field, but there is nothing there but mud and black sludge. A field of black, thick, muddy, decomposing crops. In the middle of this disgusting mess is a baby child almost glowing white, wrapped in a pure white blanket, a blanket as white as snow. I went into the mud and rescued it. I held it close to me. We were safe and out of the mud."

She wasn't sure of the meaning, but for me, it was clearly stage five, a beautiful rebirth dream. The old crops were dead. Out of decomposing black muck, the new way had appeared. The child who would save her world. Her new life. The dream is perhaps one of the most beautiful I have ever heard. If I was a painter, I would paint that image, but

I'm not, and unfortunately, neither is my client.

When I explained to her that this seemed pretty clearly a rebirth dream, she burst out in tears of joy. After which, she said: "I know you're right. I'm not the same woman I was when I started this work. I know I have changed."

"Yes, you have," I replied, "and you surely earned that remarkable dream. Don't forget it, because it is telling you where you are in this process." She agreed and understood.

In stage five, the dream sequence changes, and they find themselves in paradise, the Promised Land, because that is where they are in their life. This is when the work is coming to a close and the dreams send beautiful images of homes recently constructed, calm seas, and sun. There are often images of driving along a highway in a new, fast sports car with nothing in their way. Or they find themselves in their new dream home, which they love.

These are just some symbols and themes that my clients have shared with me as we journeyed through this process together. I hope you will begin to learn about your dreams. It is a lost art, and professional schools of psychology usually do not have one course on dreams, so working with them is not a mainstream idea for the modern therapist.

For me, I cannot imagine doing this work without the aid of the client's unconscious mind to help us along. It is a powerful ally, and it seems foolish to squander its power by refusing to honor it.

15

My Way Out of the Darkness:
Oswald and Kennedy

I had the death-rebirth experience in my thirties. I was experiencing a psychological crucifixion, stage three, in order to move to my true path, to be reborn, which I believe for now has held up. I only had to do it once. I was not a psychologist at the time, and I knew nothing about depression or anxiety. I was ignorant to most of modern psychology except for my dream work and personal reading I had been diligently doing for years.

The worse day in this process was marked by the one and only panic attack I ever had in my life. It occurred on the morning on November 22, 1991, the anniversary of John F. Kennedy's assassination.

Ironically, my invitation into this work occurred some thirteen years earlier, as I have said previously, with a request by my friend John to record and work with my dreams. My refusal led to the nightmares of Lee Harvey Oswald jumping up and down on my bed, laughing at me while the sound and feel of a tornado was blowing through the room. These nightmares occurred in 1978. That was the nightmare I called John about all those years ago that initiated my dream work. In a way, Oswald was foreshadowing the encounter with my soul that was going to come to a head on the anniversary of President Kennedy's death, about thirteen years after these nightmares had ended.

Then there is the dream and the mysterious phrase that came to me in the night: *Listen to the light of the dead*, a phrase that foreshadowed the dream of my father-in-law with the fiery sword. There was John, who was a key player in this drama as well. I had not thought of any of these things in years, but once in the darkness with journal in hand, all of these things were recalled, and I knew immediately what it meant to lose your life to save it. I knew what it meant to be crucified and born again. I understood the importance of the words *listen to the light of the dead* because not only was my father-in-law dead, the bringer of the sword, but so was Christ, the bringer of the new and holy light, but not until the death has been completed.

Now, you must admit, this is quite the coincidence, quite the synchronistic event. As I said, the soul cares nothing of time and space. Everything came together in those days surrounding the anniversary of the Kennedy assassination.

The day after this panic attack, my friend John was surprisingly back in our hometown. He lived in D.C. at this time. My wife called him and said: "Andy's in trouble. Can you come?" He was by my side immediately. He held me in his arms while I wept and sobbed out loud — not something I thought I ever would do, or could do, or ever wanted to do, but I did. He brought me the *Iron John* book that day. It helped immensely. Again, it was the perfect book at the perfect time.

John understood. He had had a similar experience a few years earlier. He reminded me that it would end; it was not as scary it felt. He was instrumental in helping me understand what was happening to me. As I said, John knows everything. I doubt he knows or remembers how important he is and was in my life. I hope he knows now.

This final piece demonstrates the slender threads that Robert Johnson talks about: the idea that the one thing that we need shows up exactly when we need it, and this leads to another connection and another. This often happens completely out of our awareness, because we do not know what the final purpose of it all is until the plan comes to fruition, which may take thirty years.

I will share a rather prophetic active imagination session of mine from this period. It is a conversation that I had with Christ. It took quite a team of people, symbols, books, doctors, and even God to get me through this treacherous process. Let's review the slowly doled-out players in timeline form.

1978 – John asks that I record my dreams. I say no.

1978 – Oswald nightmares begin almost immediately.

1978 – I surrender, record my dreams, and the nightmares stop.

1979 – *listen to the light of the dead* phrase

1979 – Fiery sword dream

1991 – November 22, 1991: first panic attack. Intense journaling and reconnection with the fiery sword dream and understanding it for the first time. Knowing how important it was to *listen to the light of the dead*. Finally left it all behind, because a prophet is not without honor except in his hometown. As Robert Lamm would say, *Goodbye*.
1996 – Recovered and began the move to the new life. *All Is Well* again.

I had the following conversation with Christ early in the period of what Bly calls Ashes and Grief. I debated whether I should include it in this book or not. In the end, I felt I had to. I had not read these words since 1991. The only other person who had read them was my wife and my friend John. This conversation has been bound up in those journals, locked away for decades. The conversation is rather prophetic. The words on these pages ended up being shockingly true. This was a dark day in 1991; this dialogue was a process born out of despair, fear, and desperation. Like, "What have I got to lose by trying this thing Morton always talks about in his books?" Below is my dialogue with Christ, much like my client's, who gave her depression the image of the blanket and felt she was speaking to God. Many of my clients report that they often have conversations similar to this during EMDR.

Christ: I've been waiting a long time under this tree for you. What took you so long? I'm always here for you.

Andy: What is happening to me? Why is all of this bad stuff happening to me?

Christ: You needed to know the darkness to appreciate and recognize the light. You need to know and appreciate the gifts you have been given. Do not fear. I will gradually breathe the life back into you, and you will be able to breathe freely again. You are missing your uniqueness. You are not using your gifts. That has to change. I had to get your attention. You now have had a taste of my suffering and the darkness I experienced. But just as I conquered it for you and all mankind, so I will help you conquer it through me. So you might recognize the choices I would have you make and not make choices for your own selfish reasons. Do not seek money. That is not your purpose. Use your gifts and the money will come. Seek money and you will never get any. Your soul is not designed to seek money, in case you didn't notice. You struggle because you're on the wrong path.

Be at peace. Just as mankind has never been the same since my death and resurrection, so you will never be the same after your experience in this dark and desolate place. You will carry this wound always, and it will glorify Me and My Father.

I will breathe the life and my light back into you. The darkness will subside in time. You will recognize it next time, and you will be able to avoid it. Your actions are correct now. Move to a more simple life and love me, and my father and my mother. Pray daily. Appreciate and recognize your gifts. I will help you and guide you, but you must take time to listen to me, and you must trust in me. Remember, I am always here. Do not be a stranger. I am here to help, but I can do nothing if you do not ask. Do not be a stranger, OK, Andy? I'm always here waiting for you.

I embraced Him. He was wearing such a soft robe. It was an embrace I never wanted to end, but it did. This experience seemed to help. It gave me hope that my troubles would eventually end, but at the time it was hard to believe that it would. I was in bad shape at that time.

Everything in this brief exchange came to pass. My life changed. I stopped seeking money but, rather, used my talents, and money has not been a problem for a long time. He was right; I still know nothing about money, but surprisingly, money is not a problem.

$$\sim \mathcal{L} \sim$$

Well, that was then, almost twenty-five years ago. I'm a pretty lucky man. Since that time, I do not remember one prayer prayed that was not answered. I'm a man whose dreams have all come true. I am married and lucky to have a beautiful wife whom I've loved for more than thirty-five years, two great kids who are working in their respective fields of study, and, of course, my old and dear friend John, who started this all for me with a phone call about a class where he was studying dreams.

It is my deepest hope that you now know how courageous one must be to engage one's soul. That therapy is a courageous thing to do. That you should turn off your cell phones, televisions, computers, and pick up a journal, get familiar with your inner self and learn how to pray. Learn how to engage and understand your inner life, your soul, your God. Make sure you are living your authentic self. Make sure you are not only on the journey you want, but the journey that God wants for you. If you do not believe in God, then be on the journey that is in alignment with your authentic self. Your ego cannot tell you this. You must look deeper.

As T. S. Eliot said, what began as a naïve exploration in my youth seems to be something I seem to understand in my sixtieth year. It's full circle for me as I look at the Thomas Merton book John purchased for me last Christmas and the rather worn *Iron John* book he gave to me all those years ago, on the other side of my desk. The cup of coffee my loving wife made for me this morning, sitting here in front of me. The desk cluttered with Morton's *Other Side of Silence* book, which looks beautifully tired, tattered, and held together with tape. Of course, *The Kingdom Within* by John Sanford is also falling apart, but I could not imagine my library without these old ancient-looking copies of these most important books. And listening to Pat Metheny during the entire process of writing this book further enriched the writing experience. Truth be told, he has written the musical score for my life.

I am so grateful to be privileged to do this work with extraordinary clients. I am grateful that they were kind enough to allow me to share a part of their stories so others may understand and become aware of this incredible process that is accelerated by EMDR. It is their hope and mine that you will all put down your smart phones, iPad, and computers, and instead begin this inner journey that perhaps will include EMDR.

I will leave you with a final dream.

Perhaps one of the most humorous and meaningful or "sense and nonsense" stage-six dreams was shared by a client who said, "Andy, I'm afraid to tell you this dream, because you might get mad." I assured her I would not get angry, because we cannot control our dreams. Her dream is below:

"I am in the living room of my new house, and I just bought a beautiful painting that cost $600. It is of a beautifully painted pastoral scene, and it will go nicely above the couch. It is strikingly beautiful; it is almost alive. Andy, you were there, too, and you said that you also had bought a painting for $600. You said that you thought yours was beautiful as well, and you showed it to me, but it was hideous. It was covered with garbage: banana peels, old cans and rotten food. It was a smelly mess."

I laughed and thought that was a great dream.

"Well, I think our work is finished. I get to keep all the ugliness and trash you had endured in your life that caused you so much anguish, and now you have a beautiful picture for the next chapter in your life. I have what is beautiful for me, and you have what is beautiful for you. A perfect dream to end our work together."

As I said in the beginning of the book, I stopped feeling like a psychologist long ago. I don't think I ever felt like a scientific-practitioner. In fact, I'm not sure what that is supposed to mean. I know I'm not a clergyman or religious scholar. I'm no holy man. A male version of a midwife, perhaps, comes closest as a companion for your inner journey.

In the end, I think this dream finally gave me my identity. After she shared this dream with me, as we both laughed, I knew at that moment exactly who and what I was. Finally, after fifty-eight years of searching, now I know; I am nothing more and nothing less than a *trash collector for the soul.*

Acknowledgements

How does one thank the people who helped bring this book to life? I don't even know where to begin. I guess I'll start with where this all began, and that was with my parents, who allowed me to live the life I wanted to live. When I was sixteen or seventeen and said I wanted to study music composition in Chicago, they didn't say, "Maybe you should pick something more practical." They had the attitude that it's your life, it's your decision, and if it's a bad decision, well, it's your bad decision, not ours. In the end, it was not a bad decision. I loved every minute of my studies at Roosevelt University studying music and being absorbed in art and surrounded by artists of all kinds. I love you, Mom and Dad, aka Sis and Skin.

I have to thank my sons, who both took time to read parts of the manuscript. My younger son, John, said: "Dad, I can't read this while I'm on a break at work. I start to cry, and I shouldn't be crying at work." My older son, Andrew, said something similar. After reading some of the chapters, he said, "Dad your book is awesome." Enough said; no greater compliment can a writer get from his sons.

Then there are the many great teachers I have had in my life. My dear friend and mentor in music school, Michael Thorn, helped me learn how to learn. After I left Chicago and returned home to Pittsburgh, Frank Cunimundo played an important role in my studies in regard to music, but more importantly, he, too, furthered my skill in understanding how to learn something that does not come easy. These two teachers taught me how to learn. I was learning music, but the skills they taught me transferred to just about any subject or activity I ever wanted to master.

In psychology, there is Dr. Richard Elmore, who was my mentor in graduate school and a longtime friend. I doubt he'll even know how much his tutelage meant to me. I do not know if I would have been able to complete graduate school without him. I also want to mention Dr. Josh Gross, Dr. David Gitlin, and Dr. Nikki Pritchet, who supervised me at Florida State University during my internship year. They taught me a lot and laid the groundwork for my understanding of just how powerful emotions are. It was during my internship at Florida State University when my father passed away. The staff was incredibly supportive. I could not have been in a better place at the time of my father's death.

Then there are the men I never met who influenced me enormously, long before I ever had a hint that I would be a psychologist or try to write a book. Morton T. Kelsey's and John A. Sanford's books opened up a new way of looking at the world and of Christ for me. Thomas Merton's books were greatly influential in the early stages of my development, and the influence of these writers continues even today. And, of course, my old friend John Whalen, who started this all for me decades ago.

I also would like to thank Dr. Sanford Drob, whose

book *Reading the Red Book: An Interpretive Guide to C. G. Jung's Liber Novus*, was indispensable as a companion to Jung's *Red Book*.

Then there is my technical support team. Chris Kridler read the manuscript and edited the first version. She made very useful corrections and suggestions; she also mentored me though some of the social media skills, of which I had none until I met her. She is also my videographer. All the videos you see on the web were created by her. Another dear friend and editor, Blair Kinney, read the final version of the manuscript and made a number of suggestions, for which I am forever grateful. She is not only an editor but spent much of her life as a therapist, so I wanted her view of the manuscript. Writing is a solitary experience. I am very grateful that Chris and Blair were willing to take the time to read and re-read the manuscript, offering many useful suggestions. Another incredibly talented woman I also wanted to thank: Nicole Bateman of The Pixel Boutique, who created my cover design and the design you see across all social media in the service of this book. If you saw the rather vague idea of what I was looking for in an image that I sent to her, and then saw this brilliant image that she created from my feeble explanation of what I wanted, you would appreciate the artistic brilliance of this skilled woman. Thank you, Nicole.

My good friend and colleague Gwen Forbes-Wolfe, who was one of the first therapists to be trained in EMDR in the state of Florida, supervised me through part of my EMDR credentialing process and has become not only a mentor but a good friend who was kind enough to read the manuscript more than once and offered very helpful suggestions. Thank you, Gwen.

There are my two colleagues that I work with every day who both invited me to join their practice. Without their confidence in my abilities and their generous invitation, I doubt this book would have ever been written. Thank you, Dr. Richard Greene and Elizabeth "Liz" Prudenti, LCSW, from the bottom of my heart. I will never forget how important that invitation was and how wonderful it has been working in the peaceful environment we have at our counseling center.

Theresa is my office manager, whom I have to thank. She is so much more than an office manager. She arranges my life, never complains, and takes care of all of the business duties for me, so I can focus on my work. I do not know what I would do without her. I doubt this book would have been written without her continued presence and support.

I have to thank all the clients who were brave enough to take their journey through a death and rebirth experience with me. I thank them all, every one of my clients, because that all taught me something. I especially want to thank those clients who allowed me to share a part of their stories in the hopes that it will encourage others to seek help when they need it, and to know there is very real and relevant help out there for those suffering.

I would also like to thank those professionals and friends who read the book and wrote the endorsements of the manuscript on the back cover. Thank you, Leslie McGuirk, Dr. Jamie Marich and John Whalen.

I wrote most of this book holed up in the Charlotte Residence Inn on South Mint Street. The staff was very friendly, helpful, and accommodating in every way, especially Stacy at the front desk. My wife was working on a project in Charlotte during the time of the writing of this book, so I would come along and spend a week every other month or so to write. It worked out very well. I can get a lot of writing done in a week with no distractions: just me in a room with a laptop, a cup of coffee, and good music playing while I write.

Finally, thank you seems a bit lame when it comes to my wife, JoAnne, who has supported me in any harebrained idea I ever wanted to try. I could not have had a better partner throughout my life. She's been the love of my life since 1975. Right or wrong, she is my alpha and omega; my life begins and ends with her, and without her, none of this seems to matter much. I don't know if that is right or wrong; I just know that it is. It is like gravity; it is the law that governs me. It is whom this book is dedicated to and whom my life is dedicated to. She is the person who makes me want to be a better man.

About the Author

Dr. Andrew Dobo was first trained in the use of EMDR more than 14 years ago. He has treated hundreds of patients and participated in literally thousands of EMDR sessions in his private psychology practice in Sebastian, Florida. He is a licensed psychologist in Florida.

Dr. Dobo is highly credentialed in the use of EMDR. He has a lifelong interest in psychology and religion. In 1977, he read a book that used Jungian theory to interpret the sayings of Jesus. John Sanford's book *The Kingdom Within* changed his view of Jesus and of psychology. He has been looking at the connections between these two disciplines his entire life. He thought he had nothing new to add to the conversation until he saw powerful changes wrought by EMDR in his clients that paralleled six distinct moments that are modeled in the Christian Passion.

Unburdening Souls at the Speed of Thought is a narrative nonfiction account of how his clients changed their lives and how their courage changed Dr. Dobo's view of his work, of himself, and of his God.

Dr. Dobo is available for workshops, retreats and presentations in subjects related to his book and work. See his website for more detailed information about the varied presentations he provides.

Follow Dr. Dobo online:

AndrewDobo.com
Twitter @EMDRmysticism
Facebook.com/emdrmysticism
LinkedIn at Andrew Dobo

Endnotes

[1] Johnson, Robert A., *Balancing Heaven and Earth: A Memoir of Visions, Dreams, and Realizations* (New York: HarperCollins Publishers, 1998), 81.

[2] Weible, Wayne, *Conversations with Mary, The Mother of Jesus* (Myrtle Beach: Weible Publishing, 1985), Part I.

[3] English Standard Version, *The Holy Bible* (Wheaton, Illinois: Crossway Bibles, 2002), Matt: 26:39.

[4] Bly, Robert, *Little Book on the Human Shadow* (San Francisco: HarperSanFrancisco, 1988), 48.

[5] Sanford, John A., *The Kingdom Within: A Study of the Inner Meaning of Jesus' Sayings* (New York: J.B. Lippincott Company, 1970), 68.

[6] Ibid., 70.

[7] Shapiro, Francine, *Eye Movement Desensitization and Reprocessing: Basic Principles, Protocols, and Procedures, Second Edition,* (New York & London: The Guilford Press, 2002), xi-xii.

[8] English Standard Version, (Wheaton, Illinois: Crossway Bibles, 2002), *The Holy Bible*, Matt. 10:34, Luke 12:51.

[9] Ibid., Matt. 10:35-6.

[10] Sanford, John A., *The Kingdom Within: A Study of the Inner Meaning of Jesus' Sayings* (New York: J.B. Lippincott Company, 1970), 83.

[11] Lewis, C.S., *Mere Christianity* (HarperCollins ebooks, 2009), location 250 of 2779.

[12] Jung, C.G., *Mysterium Coniunctionis: Collected Works Vol. 14* (Princeton, New Jersey: Princeton University Press, 1970), 252.

[13] Ibid, 2.

[14] Johnson, Robert A., *Inner Gold: Understanding Psychological Projection* (Kihei, Hawaii: Koa Books, 2008), 3.

[15] New International Version, *The Holy Bible* (Grand Rapids, Michigan: The Zondervan Corp., 1978), Matt: 26:39.

[16] Kelsey, Morton T., *Encounter With God: A Theology of Christian Experience* (Minneapolis: Bethany Fellowship Inc., 1972), 117.

[17] Jung, C.G., *The Red Book, Liber Novus* ed. Sonu Shamdasani, trans. Mark Kyburz, John Peck, and Sonu Shamdasani (New York: W.W. Norton & Company, 2009), 239b.

[18] Sanford, John A., *Mystical Christianity: A Psychological Commentary on the Gospel of John* (New York: The Crossroad Publishing Company, 1993), 42.

[19] Sanford, John A., *Healing and Wholeness* (New York: Paulist Press, 1977), 94.

[20] Kelsey, Morton T., *Resurrection: Release from Oppression* (New York: Paulist Press, 1985), 192.

[21] Kempis, Thomas A., *The Imitation of Christ* (Orleans, Massachusetts: Paraclete Press, 1982), 101.

[22] Sanford, *Healing and Wholeness* (New York: Paulist Press, 1977), 94.

[23] Bly, Robert, *Iron John: A Book About Men* (New York, NY: Addison-Wesley Publishing Company, 1990), 194.

[24] Sanford, *The Kingdom Within: A Study of the Inner Meaning of Jesus' Sayings*, (New York: J.B. Lippincott Company, 1970), 73.

[25] Ibid., 73.

[26] Ibid., 9.

[27] Sheen, Fulton J., *The Life of Christ* (New York: Image Books, 1977), 52.

[28] Sanford, *Healing and Wholeness* (New York: Paulist Press, 1977), 33.

[29] Ibid., 100.

[30] Jung, C.G., *Mysterium Coniunctionis: Collected Works Vol. 14* (Princeton, New Jersey: Princeton University Press, 1970), 353, n370.

[31] English Standard Version, *The Holy Bible*, Mark 15:34.

[32] Ibid., Matt. 16:25.

[33] Ibid., Mark 2:11.

[34] Drob, Sanford L., *Reading the Red Book: An Interpretive Guide to C.G. Jung's Liber Novus* (New Orleans: Spring Journal Books, 2012), 18.

[35] Ibid., 5, 6.

[36] Ibid., 25.

[37] Jung, C.G., *The Red Book, Liber Novus*, 236a, b, 239b.

[38] Bloom, Allan, *The Closing of the American Mind* (New York: Simon and Schuster, 1987), 67.

[39] Johnson, Robert A., *Balancing Heaven and Earth: A Memoir of Visions, Dreams, and Realizations* (New York: HarperCollins Publishers, 1998), xi.

Made in United States
Orlando, FL
29 June 2024

48444789R00136